That Thou Art

The Wisdom of the Upaniṣads

THAT THOU ART

The Wisdom of the Upaniṣads

by
Ramakrishna Puligandla

D.K. Printworld (P) Ltd.
New Delhi

Cataloging in Publication Data — DK
[Courtesy: D.K. Agencies (P) Ltd. <docinfo@dkagencies.com>]

Puligandla, R. (Ramakrishna), 1930-
That thou art : the wisdom of the Upaniṣads / by Ramakrishna Puligandla.
p. cm.
Includes bibliographical references (p.).
ISBN 13: 9788124605271
ISBN 10: 8124605270

1. Upanishads — Criticism, interpretation, etc. I. Title.

DDC 294.59218 22

ISBN13: 978-81-246-0527-1 **ISBN10: 81-246-0527-0**
First published in the USA in 2002
First Indian edition in 2009

Published and printed by :
D.K. Printworld (P) Ltd.
Regd. Office: 'Srikunj', F-52, Bali Nagar
Ramesh Nagar Metro Station, New Delhi – 110 015
Phones: (011) 2545 3975; 2546 6019; *Fax*: (011) 2546 5926
E-mail: dkprintworld@vsnl.net
Website: www.dkprintworld.com

To

my wife Janaki
with
Love and Gratifude

". . . Some simple folk think that they will see God as if He were standing there and they here. It is not so. God and I, we are one."
— Meister Eckhart

"Knowledge is a means to freedom. . . . Philosophy, *brahma-vidyā* (knowledge of *Brahman*), is the pursuit of wisdom by a way of life."
— S. Radhakrishnan

"The Upaniṣads provide the most rewarding and the most elevating reading the world has to offer. It has been the consolation of my life and will be my consolation when I come to die."
— Arthur Schopenhauer

"The striving of all the scholars of Vedānta was really to assimilate this grandest of all thoughts. . . . Consciousness is a singular of which the plural is unknown."

— Erwin Schrodinger

"Religions, which have their different standpoints, each claim them (the Upaniṣads) for their support."

— Rabindranath Tagore

"Nothing that has disturbed the schools to controversy escaped their (the Upaniṣadic sages') notice."
— W.B. Yeats

". . . Then we will join, from our transoceanic distance, in the world-reverberating jungle roar of India's wisdom."

— Heinrich Zimmer

Foreword

IN one of the greatest of the ancient Hindu Upaniṣads, the *Kaṭha,* the story is told of a father who is giving away all of his personal possessions as sacrificial gifts. His son, a brāhmaṇa youth named Naciketā, disturbed by his father's action, asks, "Father, to whom will you give me?" Twice he asks his father the same question and twice he receives no answer. He then asks a third time, "Father, to whom will you give me?" In anger the father cries out, "I will give you to Death!" In sorrow but ever-obedient to his father's wrathful order the youth now journeys, alone and fearful, to the dark and foreboding underworld of the dead. Upon arrival he discovers that the Lord of the dead, the dreaded Yama, is absent. And Yama remains absent for three days. And for three days the reluctant and anxious guest remains without food, comfort and his host.

Finally, Lord Yama returns and is upset at finding a guest in his house, a brāhmaṇa guest who has been waiting for three days. The ancient laws of hospitality decree that since the host, Lord Yama, has erred in keeping his guest, Naciketā, waiting, he now owes that guest a boon, an apologetic gift, because of his tardiness. To make amends Death grants the young brāhmaṇa three wishes and it is those that form the substance of this most appealing and insightful liberation myth of all of the Upaniṣads.

Naciketā accepts Lord Yama's apology and, though initially reluctant, begins with his three requests. First, he wishes to be returned to life and to his father with the latter's anger now dispelled. Second, he wishes to understand the laying of the brick altar steps for a fire sacrifice, a ritual that leads the sacrificer to heaven. While Yama quickly grants both of these boons, the next and last wish is not so readily bestowed. Third, Naciketā wishes to know what happens to a man after death. Yama at first refuses outright to answer; he then demurs and hems and haws trying to put the boy off. He has, in a sense, already answered the third request by the responses that he gave to the first two requests: The first stated that after death a man may be reborn to life, and the second said that after death a man may be reborn to heaven. But neither of these answers is the one that Naciketā now seeks, and Lord Yama knows it. That third answer lies at a deeper level of understanding and insight, and the answer to that third question in the myth of the *Kaṭha* is what the Upaniṣads are really all about.

But now a new issue has arisen. Is Naciketā fully qualified as a student of sacred knowledge to receive an answer to this third query? Seeking to test his worthiness to receive that knowledge, Lord Yama tempts the youth with promises of wealth, a long life, sons, grandsons, cattle, horses, gold, lovely maidens, chariots and lutes. Naciketā responds by refusing these pleasures saying that all of these belong ultimately to decay and death and to Lord Yama. Satisfied that his young pupil is indeed qualified to hear the secret teachings, to understand the higher knowledge and to grasp its sacred wisdom, Death at last relents and offers to give the real answer to Naciketā's third question. That question was:

> Some say a man exists when dead, others that he exists not.
> This I would know, when a man dies what then?
>
> — *Kaṭha Upaniṣad* I.20

The remainder of the *Kaṭha* then explores and analyzes and ultimately answers this most fundamental of all human questions by a lengthy discourse on this "supreme secret" (*Kaṭha Upaniṣad* III.17).

The *Kaṭha Upaniṣad* was composed some time in the seventh

or sixth century BCE. and is probably the most poetic, the most mysterious, the most lyrical and beautiful, the most religious and philosophical, of some 200 of these great compositions to which we give the name "Upaniṣad." Having satisfied himself that Naciketā is worthy to become his *celā*, pupil, Lord Yama takes on the role of *guru*, master, and begins the sacred instruction by teaching Naciketā what it is that survives the death of the body. That Survivor, he states, is the *ātman*, the true Self, and that Self is *Brahman*, the Holy Power of the Universe, the *oṁ*, the sacred sonant symbol of ultimate reality. In one of the most moving Sanskrit passages in the Upaniṣads, Lord Yama tells Naciketā about this ultimately real Self:

> That which is hard to see,
> That which is hidden, set in the secret place of the heart,
> That which dwells in the depths of you,
> That which is really God, your true teacher,
> That which through *yoga*-study one comes to see,
> That you finally come to by leaving behind both joy and sorrow, good and evil, the best and the pleasant, opinion and ignorance. — *Kaṭha Upaniṣad* II.12

Three of the central themes of the Upaniṣads have been presented in this passage: The true Self is God; the true Self is hidden deep within the heart of all; and this Self can be known by abandoning, or by transcending, ordinary and common emotions and feelings.

Naciketā questions further his *guru*, and Lord Yama responds by identifying two remaining themes: There is an identity between *oṁ*, *Brahman* and that indwelling Self or *ātman*; and fifth, and finally, there is a liberating power that comes to him who truly knows that identity:

> That *oṁ* is *Brahman*, the spiritual power, the holy power of the universe.
> Knowing *oṁ* whatever one desires is his.
> *oṁ* is the chief and only support of the universe.

> Knowing that support one becomes great in the world of *Brahman*.

Lord Yama returns then to his *celā*'s third boon, his third question, and answers it clearly, succinctly and finally. You are that holy sound, you are that sacred Power, you are the supreme Self:

> That *oṁ* dwells in you Naciketā.
> It is not born. It does not die.
> It has not come from anywhere. It has not become anyone.
> Unborn, constant, eternal, the first and the last.
> It dies not when the body dies.
> That is what you searched for. — *Kaṭha Upaniṣad* II.16-18

These five themes, that the Self is real, that It lies within each of us, that It can be known through discipline and instruction, that It is identical with *Brahman* and *oṁ*, and that knowing that transcendent *Brahman* is identical to immanent *ātman*, liberates oneself forever and leads to ultimate happiness. These are the essential and central themes of all the Upaniṣads.

The *Kaṭha Upaniṣad* concludes with a passage tying all these themes together, a passage that has become all-too-familiar in the world's great sacred literature. Lord Yama says to his "beloved" disciple:

> If the slayer thinks that he slays,
> If the slain thinks himself slain,
> Both of these understand not.
> This One, this Self, neither slays nor is It slain.
> Smaller than the smallest, greater than the greatest
> Is this *Brahman*, this *oṁ*, this *ātman* that is set in the heart of every creature here. — *Kaṭha Upaniṣad* II.19-20

The three syllables of the word *upaniṣad* together mean "to sit down near," to sit so close that these secret teachings could be whispered by the *guru* into the *celā's* ear. R. Puligandla now becomes the *guru* for the reader in his magnificent introduction to the philosophy and religion of these sacred compositions. I know the reader will find Puligandla's instruction as liberating as it was for this reader. But let this classic entreaty from the oldest Upaniṣad close this foreword to Puligandla's wonderful introduction to the Upaniṣads:

> From the unreal lead me to the real,
> From darkness lead me to light,
> From death lead me to immortality.
> — *Bṛhadāraṇyaka Upaniṣad* I.3.28

A. L. Herman
Professor Emeritus of Philosophy

The author is most grateful to the Vedanta Society of Southern California for permitting him to quote from *The Upaniṣads: Breath of the Eternal* (The principal texts selected and translated from the original Sanskrit, by Swami Prabhavānanda and Frederick Manchester, 1975). The author is most thankful to Professor S.V. Bokil, Editor-in-Chief, *Indian Philosophical Quarterly*, for granting permission to reproduce parts of the author's article that appeared in the journal in 1999.

Preface

THIS book is for all people who are interested in and committed to serious quest for liberating knowledge and hence for true freedom, wisdom, peace, and joy, irrespective of ethnic, religious, national, and political identifications. There has been for some time now in the West increasing interest in the religious quest, and more than a few Westerners have been led in their quest to study and practise the traditions of India and China — Vedānta, Buddhism, Taoism, Ch'an Buddhism ("Zen Buddhism" in Japan), and so on. There has been an enhanced interest in the mystical pursuit, and there are Westerners who study and practise Yoga, recognized and recommended by even Western doctors and health-care specialists and providers. There are Westerners who systematically practise some form or other of meditation, including the well-known Transcendental Meditation. This book fills a timely need on behalf of anyone who is earnestly yearning to discover her or his true being and hence ultimate reality, and clearly understand the status and nature of the being of the world. In this connection, it is important to note that the mystical pursuit is not confined to the Indian and Chinese traditions; on the contrary, it was, is, and will be in all civilizations, including the non-literate and pre-literate. There have always been mystics in the Jewish, Christian, and Islamic traditions. However, mysticism always occupied a marginal and peripheral position in these traditions, unlike the Indian and Chinese, characterized by the centrality of the mystical quest. This book is to inspire people to discover and practise the mystical quest as formulated in their own traditions;

for all mystical pursuits lead to the same realization. The Upaniṣads are mystical works *par excellence* and hence have the power to awaken everyone to the mystical quest. This is the ultimate justification for my writing this book.

There are innumerable works, ancient, modern, and contemporary, on the Upaniṣads. If so, why another book? Almost all the books on the Upaniṣads are too voluminous and academic and therefore do not command the attention of the intelligent and inquiring segment of the general public. Accordingly, the sole reason for my writing this book is to make available and accessible a book to the sector of the general public I alluded to above. Thus anyone who is not an academic specialist but genuinely and seriously interested in inquiring into the self, the world, God, and the ultimate reality and thereby the meaning and purpose of life will find this book a clear response in her or his quest for reality and wisdom. This does not, however, mean that the book lacks rigour, precision, and textual exactitude; rather, it means that there is nothing in it that an academician can find fault with and that the essence of the Upaniṣadic teaching and wisdom is conveyed without the scholarly jargon, which, while it certainly has its place — the academia — will only serve to confuse, bewilder, discourage, and dishearten the inquiring, searching, and questing lay reader. In short, the book is clean and tight from the scholarly standpoint and at the same time it is informative, easily readable, and yet one unfailingly gets the meaning and message (of the Upaniṣadic seers and sages, *ṛṣis*, in Sanskrit). I have deliberately avoided burdening the reader with footnotes, the typical scholarly embellishments, since my prime concern here is to get the reader to clearly grasp and *examine* the Upaniṣadic teaching and arrive at her or his own verdict. Even if the reader does not agree with me, she is now more informed and better educated than when she began reading the book. I wish to stimulate, provoke, and inspire the reader to inquire and never to settle for second-hand truth. Only truth, certifiable through one's own, direct, existential, and authentic experience, is worthy of the title "first-hand truth." All else is a product of concepts, images, and projections — in short, of conditioning — lacking the power to radically transform the human being. If I am even moderately successful in realizing this goal — inspiring the reader to inquire — I will have been more than rewarded.

It is not my purpose in this book to discuss and comment on each of the Upaniṣads; rather, my purpose is to provide the essence — the heart — of the Upaniṣadic teaching, as can be gathered from all the principal Upaniṣads and elaborate upon the meaning and significance of the central teaching. If I were to discuss each of the Upaniṣads in detail, this book would be a work for the academics and not for the readership I intend it for. I should be most gratified, if readers of the book feel sufficiently inspired to read the Upaniṣads themselves. There can be no greater reward for an author.

However, that I shall not discuss each of the Upaniṣads does not, at all, mean that the reader will be missing something essential, crucial, and most significant and valuable of the Upaniṣadic teaching and wisdom; let me assure the reader that such is not the case, for what I propose to offer here is the very heart-beat of the Upaniṣadic teaching. Everything at the core of this teaching is presented in an easily readable, understandable, and hence enjoyable manner and style. The reader will only miss the burden and unpleasant task of going through a plethora of footnotes, references, and other academic decorations, not at all necessary or indispensable for clearly and authentically communicating the grand vision and fundamental message of the Upaniṣads. I shall quote the Upaniṣadic texts only when necessary, in documenting the central concepts and propositions. I also shall provide a relevant bibliography — a list of references, for purposes of further study and reflection.

Sanskrit words will be used, and once the reader understands a concept, she will more or less automatically (spontaneously!) remember the Sanskrit word or phrase corresponding to the concept. In any case, I shall employ the minimum possible number of Sanskrit words and phrases; and even when I provide the Sanskrit terms in parentheses, it is not important for the reader to remember them; rather, what is of paramount importance is that the reader clearly and fully grasp the concept and the message under discussion. I shall now move on to address myself to the task at hand.

Contents

	Foreword	vii
	Preface	xiii
	Acknowledgements	xviii
	Introduction	1
1.	The Central Upaniṣadic Insights	9
2.	Clarification and Discussion	23
3.	Philosophical Significance	53
4.	Philosophical Significance (Continued)	69
5.	Religious Significance	87
6.	Concluding Remarks and Reflections	111
	Glossary	125
	Bibliography	135
	Index	143

Acknowledgements

I WISH to thank all of my former students who, through their relentlessly inquiring minds, forced me to think and re-think, over a period of more than three decades, in order to satisfactorily answer their deepest and most thoughtful questions and objections in regard to the Upaniṣadic teaching and wisdom. There could be no greater reward for a teacher than having students who challenge him at every twist and turn and demand total clarity and consistency.

I am especially thankful to my friend and former student and attorney-at-law, Ms Lucinda Haddad Hopkins, for enthusiastically suggesting and unfailingly encouraging me to write this book. I am also in no small measure indebted to her for her perusal of the manuscript and constructive comments and observations.

I am equally thankful to my fellow-scholars in the U.S.A., Europe, India, China, and Japan for generously sharing with me over the years their mastery, expertise, and insights.

I am most grateful to Professor Arthur L. Herman, of the University of Wisconsin, an original thinker and a distinguished authority on Indian thought and tradition, for deeming this work worthy of his foreword.

Any faults that may yet remain are, of course, entirely my own.

R. Puligandla

Introduction

WHAT exactly are the Upaniṣads? In order to clearly answer this question, we need to understand what is known as "the Vedic background" and therewith the evolution of ideas from this background into the central Upaniṣadic insights.

The Vedas, by scholarly consensus, are the oldest (1500–800 BCE) among the sacred writings and scriptures of the world. Before we go on, an important clarification is to be made concerning the word "scripture." "Scripture" is a Western concept, belonging to the Semitic-based traditions — the Jewish, Christian, and Islamic — meaning the word of God. The Vedas are not the word of God; that is, they are not to be thought of as revealed by God to the human being. Nevertheless, they can be understood as revelation, in the sense of Truth revealing Itself to Itself; simply put, Truth which reveals Itself and to whom It is revealed are one and the same. In the light of these considerations, the Vedas are most correctly referred to as Śruti, meaning that which is directly heard, as different from Smṛti, that which is remembered as the teachings of the ancient seers and sages. "Sacred writings of Hinduism" is thus the most appropriate way of referring to the Vedas. They are the source of the sacred knowledge and wisdom of orthodox Hinduism in its various forms. The term "Veda" is etymologically related to the English "wit," meaning knowledge. (It surely is of interest to note here that the English words "witch" and "wicca" originally referred to a person of knowledge and wisdom, long before witches and witchcraft fell into disrepute and it became customary and matter-of-fact to burn at the stake persons accused of witch-crafting. These observations are not meant to suggest that the Vedas have something to do with witchcraft; rather, the intent of these remarks is to call attention to the linguistic fact of meanings; in particular, the meaning of "Veda," knowledge. Such coincidence of meaning should not be surprising, for Sanskrit is an ancient Indo-European tongue and no wonder there is overlap of vocabularies between Sanskrit and English). The Vedas are regarded by Hindus as divine in origin and not the work of human authors (*apauriṣeya*); accordingly, they are looked upon as timeless and eternal. This is not to deny that at a certain time in human history the Vedas acquired a specific verbal form, oral or written; it only means that the truths proclaimed by the Vedas are eternal truths and in no way dependent upon the manner, time, and place of their recording.

The Vedas are four in number: the *Ṛg*, the *Sāma*, the *Yajūr*, and the *Atharva*. Each of these may be regarded as consisting of four parts, the first three pertaining to rituals and sanctions, and the last to knowledge, philosophic and transcendental. For this reason, the first three parts together are known as *karma-kāṇḍa* (the part pertaining to practical matters, including ethics and codes of conduct), and the last as *jñāna-kāṇḍa* (the part pertaining to knowledge). The four parts of each Veda are as follows:

1. the Saṁhitās,
2. the Brāhmaṇas,
3. the Āraṇyakas, and
4. the Upaniṣads.

We may note here that the term "Upaniṣad" has many meanings, three of which are as follows:

(a) sitting close to the teacher and listening to him as he expounds the teachings,

(b) that which destroys ignorance and illusion and brings one knowledge of liberating truth and hence of ultimate reality, and

(c) secret teaching, for in the ancient Vedic tradition the teachings of the Upaniṣads were very closely guarded and given only to those whom the teacher judged worthy of receiving them.

The Saṁhitās are hymns and chants in praise of various nature-gods, such as air (Vāyu), fire (Agni), rain (Parjanya), thunder (Indra), sun (Mitra), and so on. The hymns are sung in order to please the gods and thereby receive from them the blessings of worldly goods such as health, wealth, power, and fame. The Brāhmaṇas are manuals for performing various kinds of rituals and ceremonies as well as guides for the conduct of everyday life. They describe in detail the procedures for performing different rituals for pleasing different gods, as well as the kinds of sacrifices to be offered to them; they also lay down the rules of conduct and duties and obligations of human beings towards each other. It is worth pointing out that the undue emphasis on the performance of rites, ceremonies, and duties has in course of time resulted in the degradation of religious consciousness: the mere chanting of certain words, the performance of certain rites, and conducting oneself in certain ways have replaced genuine religious consciousness. Thus empty utterances and mechanical gestures have themselves come to be regarded as constituting the core of religious life. From such degeneration it is but a short step to the emergence of an all-powerful priestly class and therewith the rigid institutionalization of religion. However, these remarks are not to be construed as implying that the Brāhmaṇas are wholly devoid of anything valuable. Indeed, they emphasize self-control and exhort people to cultivate love, kindness, and charity towards all living beings, including non-human animals. Further, the Brāhmaṇas forbid murder, theft, greed, and jealousy. The Brāhmaṇas therefore surely deserve to be commended for their lofty ethical teachings. Nevertheless, their excessive emphasis on rituals and ceremonies did result in the gradual eclipse of genuine and sublime religious consciousness.

Like the Brāhmaṇas, the Āraṇyakas (literally "forest treatises") deal with rites and ceremonies. But, unlike the Brāhmaṇas, they go beyond rites and ceremonies to remind the human being that true and liberating knowledge and wisdom does not consist in the mere performance of rituals and ceremonies but in spiritual insight into ultimate reality. The Āraṇyakas call upon us to inquire into and grasp the spiritual significance behind the Vedic sanctions, rituals, and ceremonies. In other words, the Āraṇyakas are the transition from the outward symbols to the inner reality. In this manner, the Āraṇyakas pave the path to the Upaniṣads, the flower of Vedic wisdom.

Before proceeding to a discussion of the central insights of the Upaniṣads, let us briefly present the evolution of the concepts of nature, man, God, and ultimate reality in the Saṁhitās, the Brāhmaṇas, and the Āraṇyakas. The idea permeating the *Ṛgveda* is that nature in all of its diversity and multiplicity is not a chaos but is governed by a basic cosmic law (*ṛta*). To this law are subject not only all natural phenomena, such as the movements of the planets and the generation, growth, decay, and death of organisms, but also truth and justice, the latter being ineluctably dependent upon the former (for how can justice be served if truth is not known?). At this stage of the Vedic thought, many gods are said to exist; that is, the Vedas *seem* to subscribe to polytheism, belief in many gods. Hymns are sung in praise of each god in order to receive his favours; but on closer examination it turns out that each god is praised in the respective hymns as the highest and supreme lord and creator and ruler of the universe. How does one make sense of this paradoxical and contradictory belief and attitude? Max Müller, the great Indologist of the nineteenth century, distinguished this kind of belief and attitude from polytheism and referred to it as "henotheism." Thus, while belief in many gods is common to polytheism and henotheism, only the latter holds that each god is the highest and supreme. One might argue that the elevation of each god to the highest status is either romantic hyperbole or an act of opportunistic exaggeration and sycophancy motivated by selfish ends and, consequently, that the henotheism of the Vedas is really no different from polytheism. Such a view is not tenable, however; for we have good reasons to believe that the Vedic exaltation of each god to the supreme status is governed by the belief and conviction that the different gods are *manifestations* of *one single* underlying reality: "To what is one, sages give many a title: they call it, Agni, Yama, Mātarisvan" (*Ṛgveda*, I.164.46, from R.T.H. Griffith, *The Hymns of the Ṛgveda*, Banaras: E.J. Lazarus & Company, 3rd edn., 1920-26). In the light of this utterance, it is neither absurd nor paradoxical to think of each god as the most high and supreme. This interpretation is firmly grounded in and substantiated by the explicit declaration of the unity of all existence. Thus, according to the celebrated hymn known as the Puruṣa-Sūkta,

> Thousand-headed was the *puruṣa* (person or the human being personified), thousand-eyed, thousand-footed. He embraced the earth on all sides, and stood beyond the breadth of ten fingers.
>
> The *puruṣa* is this all, that which was and which shall be. He is Lord of immortality, which he grows beyond through (sacrificial) food.
>
> Such is his greatness, and still greater than that is the *puruṣa*. One-fourth of him is all beings. The three-fourths of him is the immortal in Heaven.
>
> Three-fourths on high rose the *puruṣa*. One fourth of him arose here (on the earth). Thence in all directions he spread abroad, as that which eats and that which eats not.
>
> — *Ṛgveda* X.90.1-4, from Edward J. Thomas, *Vedic Hymns, Wisdom of the East*, Oxford University Press, 1923

It is clear that the theme of this hymn is the unity of all existence, inorganic as well as organic. Such unity is expressed by the Vedic seers in their grand visual imagery, in the form of what they call "the *Puruṣa*." According to this hymn, "the *Puruṣa*" is not to be equated with the universe, for not only does he pervade the universe but he is also beyond it. In philosophical terms, the supreme reality is both immanent and transcendent — immanent, because it pervades all existence, thereby rendering it a unity; transcendent, because it is not exhausted by existence but goes beyond it. In religious terms, God, while pervading the universe, is also more than the universe. In other words, the Vedic conception of God is not pantheistic but panentheistic (pantheism is the view that God and the universe are identical, whereas panentheism is the view that God is not exhausted by the universe but is greater than it and transcends it). It is in this manner, then, that the Vedic vision of the unity of existence leads to panentheism, which may be alternatively expressed by saying that the totality of existence is *in* God but *not equal* to God.

We have seen that the *Ṛgveda* refers to the supreme reality underlying and unifying all existence by the term *puruṣa* (person or the human being personified). The question now arises, Is this conception of ultimate reality anthropomorphic? The Vedic answer to this question is a clear "No," for the famous hymn of creation, also known as Nāsadīya-Sūkta, Hymn of Negation, unequivocally declares that ultimate reality (the *Puruṣa*) is not only impersonal but beyond all names and forms, and hence is inexpressible and indescribable:

> Non-being then existed not nor being
> There was no air, nor sky that is beyond it
> What was concealed? Wherein? In whose protection?
> And was there deep unfathomable water?
>
> Who knows for certain? Who shall here declare it?
> Whence was it born, and whence came this creation?
> The gods were born after this world's creation;
> Then who can know from whence it has arisen?
>
> None knoweth whence creation has arisen;
> And whether he has or has not produced it;
> He who surveys it in the highest heaven,
> He only knows, or haply he may know not.
>
> — *Ṛgveda* X.I29.1, 6, 7, from A.A. Macdonell,
> *Hymns from the Ṛgveda,* OUP, 1922

It is clear that according to this hymn all existence is the manifestation of a single ultimate reality, which, being beyond thoughts and words, is indescribable, indeterminate, and absolute. To be sure, this grand and profound conception of ultimate reality is not grounded in discursive, philosophical speculation but in the loftiest of poetic, mystical, intuitive insights. It is also worth noting that this vision of reality also goes beyond all gods to the primordial ground of all existence. It goes beyond polytheism and monotheism to pure non-dualism. Such a vision is the inspiration of all the Upaniṣads as well as all the subsequent philosophical speculations of the Vedāntic schools. To sum up, then, even the extra-Upaniṣadic Vedic literature contains the highest non-dualistic vision of reality. In the light of this, it would be a grave error to think, as many do, that the religious consciousness informing the Vedic hymns is at best polytheism and at worst animism and nature worship. Through their sublime and lofty vision of ultimate reality, the Vedic hymns reveal a profound mystical consciousness.

1

The Central Upaniṣadic Insights

AS POINTED out in the last chapter, the Upaniṣads are the last — concluding — parts of the Vedas and are the culmination of the Vedic knowledge and wisdom. For this reason, the Upaniṣads are also referred to as *Vedānta* (*Veda+anta, anta* meaning end, conclusion). We do not know how many Upaniṣads existed originally. One hundred and eight Upaniṣads have survived and come down to us. Some of them are composed in prose, others in verse, and still others partly in one and partly in the other. The style of the Upaniṣads is direct, forceful, aphoristic, and often didactic and dialogic. We are wholly in the dark as to the particular persons who authored the Upaniṣads and exactly when. We do know, however, that the people who composed them called themselves "Vedic Aryans" and their language was Sanskrit. It is of interest to note here that it was a common custom in ancient India for authors to remain anonymous. The reason for this was their strong conviction that what mattered was the truths proclaimed and not the identity or history of the authors, who looked upon themselves as merely the vehicles for communicating impersonal and eternal truths. Thus the names of the great sages whose extraordinary insights are the Upaniṣads forever remain a mystery.

Of the hundred and eight extant Upaniṣads, ten have come to be regarded as the cream of the Upaniṣadic teachings. They are as follows: *Īśa, Kena, Kaṭha, Praśna, Muṇḍaka, Māṇḍūkya, Chāndogya, Bṛhadāraṇyaka, Aitareya,* and *Taittirīya.* These Upaniṣads are the subject of innumerable commentaries, ancient, modern, and contemporary. The commentaries of Śaṅkara, the founder of the school of Advaita-Vedānta, are by far the most important and influential.

It is important to bear in mind that the Upaniṣads are not to be thought of as systematic philosophical treatises, although they deal with the most profound, subtle, and sublime philosophical concepts and questions. The authors of the Upaniṣads did not look upon themselves as builders of philosophical systems, but as men and women conveying their own experiences of and insights into reality. Consequently, it would be fruitless to look in the Upaniṣads for a systematic, coherent, logical development of ideas. One should be prepared to encounter apparent inconsistencies, undue emphasis on one idea here and another there, and sometimes even wholly unconnected digressions in the articulation of a given idea or theme. Further, the Upaniṣads are sometimes repetitious. The same idea may be dealt with in several places in more or less the same fashion. How do we account for this peculiar character of the style and texture of the Upaniṣads? One answer is that they are not the work of a single author, but the accumulation of the expressions and articulations of the insights and experiences of different men and women over a long period of time. Another explanation for the non-systematic character of the Upaniṣads is that their authors were concerned not so much with minutiae as with providing a comprehensive account of their vision and insights. In short, their attention was not upon parts but on the whole. Thus the Upaniṣads abound in terse, aphoristic, and epigrammatic statements with inspiring meanings. Scintillating significance and dynamic intuition are packed into short and powerful utterances. Precisely for these reasons the Upaniṣads give rise to diverse interpretations. This is not to say that there is no unity in the Upaniṣads. Quite the contrary, there are some fundamental concepts and meanings which run through all the Upaniṣads, thereby bestowing unity in their content. As such, the various commentaries, no matter what their differences, share these fundamental concepts and propositions, which we shall now present.

Brahman

When the ancient sages turned their gaze on the external world, they found it to be one of ceaseless change. The birth, growth, decay, and death of the stupendous variety of life-forms, the waxing and waning of the moon, the coming and going of seasons, the appearance and disappearance of stars, all suggested to them that change and transience permeate the entire external world. Nothing seems to remain the same. Awed by the panorama of perennial change and impermanence around them, the sages asked: Is this all that there is to the world, a mere passing, fleeting show? Is there nothing but change, impermanence, birth, growth, and death? Or is there a reality amidst and behind the changing world that is timeless and eternal? They answered these questions affirmatively by saying that there is indeed a reality timeless and eternal in the midst of the changing world. That reality they called *Brahman*. (The term *Brahman* derives from the root√*bṛh* meaning to burst forth. This root-meaning underlies the philosophic conception of *Brahman* as the primordial reality spontaneously bursting forth as the world of variety and multiplicity). It is of the utmost importance to note that the existence of the world of change itself is what has suggested to the seers the notion of the eternal *Brahman*. For in the absence of any change, how could one be led to the idea of the timeless and eternal? But soon they are confronted with the pressing questions: What is the relation between the eternal *Brahman* and the changing world? Are *Brahman* and the world two different realities? Or are they one and the same? The answers to these questions are at once a clarification of the concepts *Brahman* and "world."

According to the Upaniṣads, *Brahman* is the imperishable and timeless reality underlying every sector and facet of the world of change. Thus,

> In the heart of all things, of whatever there is in the universe, dwells the Lord. — *Īśa* 1*

This is the truth of *Brahman* in relation to nature:
whether in the flash of lightning, or in the wink of
the eyes, the power that is shown is the power of *Brahman*
— *Kena* IV.4

This is the truth of *Brahman* in relation to men:
in the motions of the mind, the power that
is shown is the power of *Brahman.* — *Kena* IV.5

The Imperishable is the Real. As sparks innumerable fly
upward from a blazing fire, so from the depths of the
Imperishable arise all things. To the depths of the
Imperishable they again descend. — *Muṇḍaka* II.i.1

Self-luminous is that Being, and formless. He dwells within
all and without all. He is unborn, pure, greater than
the greatest, without breath, without mind. — *Muṇḍaka* II.i.2

It should be clear from these passages that *Brahman* is the selfsame power, the imperishable reality behind the world of ceaseless change. At this stage, the Upaniṣadic conception of reality seems to be dualistic — the changing world on the one hand and the imperishable *Brahman* on the other. But such a view is wholly mistaken, for the Upaniṣads untiringly declare that *Brahman* is the *sole* reality. Just as different objects made of clay are different from each other only in name and form, so also the world of change is a world of names and forms only, while its substance alone is the reality, the eternal and imperishable *Brahman:* "In words or speech alone the modification (change) originates and exists. In reality there is no such thing as modification. It is merely a name, and the clay alone is real" (*Chāndogya* IV.i.4). These sayings make it unmistakably clear that the Upaniṣadic conception of reality, far from being one of dualism constituted of the changing world

---

* (**Note:** All the passages from Upaniṣads quoted in this work are from *The Upaniṣads: Breath of the Eternal,* tr. Swami Prabhavānanda and Frederick Manchester, New York: Mentor, 1975.)

and the eternal *Brahman*, is thoroughgoingly non-dualistic: *Brahman* is the sole reality.

Brahman, unlike the world of our senses and intellect, is beyond names and forms. Consequently, nothing can be positively affirmed of *Brahman;* one can only say what *Brahman* is not. All description is relation, and since there can be nothing besides *Brahman*, *Brahman* cannot be described. Yet *Brahman* is the power that pervades all existence. This point is poignantly expressed by the Upaniṣads as follows:

> *Brahman* is he whom speech cannot express, and from whom the mind, unable to reach him, comes away baffled.
>
> — *Taittirīya* II.4

> That which cannot be expressed in words but by which the tongue speaks — know that to be *Brahman. Brahman* is not the being who is worshipped of men. — *Kena* I.5

> That which is not comprehended by the mind but by which the mind comprehends — know that to be *Brahman. Brahman* is not the being worshipped of men. — *Kena* I.6

> That which is not seen by the eye but by which the eye sees — know that to be *Brahman. Brahman* is not the being worshipped of men. — *Kena* I.7

> That which is not drawn by the breath but by which the breath is drawn — know that to be *Brahman. Brahman* is not the being worshipped of men. — *Kena* I.9

Thus *Brahman* is the inexpressible, invisible, inaudible, and unthinkable ground of all existence. *Brahman* is neither a he nor a she but That (*Tat*). *Brahman* is not to be mistaken for and identified with any God or gods people worship. *Brahman* can never be captured by the senses or intellect, but can only be experienced in a flash of non-dual mystical intuition (*prajñā*).

To sum up, there are no two realities, the world of change

and the eternal *Brahman*. Rather, there is one and only one reality, the imperishable and inexpressible *Brahman*. The world of our senses and intellect is merely a world of names and forms having no reality apart from *Brahman*. It is indeed *Brahman* itself appearing to us through the multiplicity of names and forms. Clay is one reality, although it may manifest itself through different names and forms.

Ātman

When the Upaniṣadic sages turned their attention inward, they found there a vast world, which, like the external world, is one of incessant change. The inner world is a phantasmagoria of sensations, perceptions, thoughts, emotions, images, memories, feelings, and so on. There seemed to be nothing there that was permanent and enduring. They then asked: Is the inner world just a passing phenomenon of shifting and fleeting things? Or is there some reality in it that is eternal and imperishable? They answered again that there is indeed a reality amidst and behind the inner world of tumult and turmoil that is timeless and everlasting. That reality they called *ātman,* the silent, imperishable witness of all change. (In all likelihood, the original meaning of *ātman* is breath; and since breath is the essence of life, the term has been subsequently used to signify the essential part or quality of anything. Thus in its philosophic sense *ātman* means the inmost self of the human being as well as of the universe. It is of interest to note that the German word *atmen* means to breathe). *Ātman* is the inmost self of the human being and is not to be confused with the empirical ego (*jīva*), which, far from being the timeless silent witness, is subject to unceasing change. It is the empirical ego that we are ordinarily aware of and call "self" and study in psychological laboratories. That the empirical ego is not to be mistaken for the *ātman* is clear from the following passage:

> As a lump of salt when thrown into water melts away and the lump cannot be taken out, but wherever we taste the water it

> tastes salty, even so, O Maitreyī, the individual self, dissolved, is the Eternal — pure consciousness, infinite and transcendent. Individuality arises by identification of the Self, through ignorance, with the elements; and with the disappearance of consciousness of the many, in divine illumination, it disappears. Where there is consciousness of the Self, individuality is no more. — *Bṛhadāraṇyaka* II.iv.12

Ātman is pure spirit, unborn, uncreated, undying, eternal, and immortal:

> Ah, Maitreyī, my beloved, the Intelligence which reveals all — by that shall it be revealed. By whom shall the Knower be known? The Self is described as *not this, not that*. It is incomprehensible, for it cannot be comprehended; undecaying, for it never decays; unattached, for it never attaches itself; unbound, for it is never bound.
> — *Bṛhadāraṇyaka* II.iv.14

Further, *ātman* exists not just in the human being but in all beings, animate as well as inanimate — seas and stars, trees and thunder, birds and beasts, and so on. In the heart of all things, of whatever there is in the universe, dwells the Self:

> The Self is the Lord of all beings. As the spokes are held together in the hub and in the felly of a wheel, just so all beings, all creatures, all gods, all worlds, all lives, are held together in the Self. — *Bṛhadāraṇyaka* II.v.15

The phenomenal world — the world of our senses and mind — is a hierarchy of beings, with the inanimate at one end and the human being at the other. But — this is the important point — *ātman* is present in all beings, irrespective of their places in the hierarchy. Put differently, every existent is at the core spiritual.

From what has been said thus far, it should be clear to the reader that according to the Upaniṣads there is the *ātman* on the one hand and the *Brahman* on the other. *Brahman* is the substance of all existence — the imperishable reality, of which the world of change is a mere manifestation through names and forms. *Ātman* is the eternal, silent witness in all beings; it is the pure spirit, all-pervading. Further, both *ātman* and *Brahman,* being beyond names and forms, are imperceivable, inconceivable, and inexpressible and are to be experienced only in non-dual intuition — *prajñā.* Both are unborn, uncreated, undying, eternal, and immortal. There arise now two questions: Are *ātman* and *Brahman* two different realities, the former underlying the inner world, and the latter the outer? What is the relation between *ātman* and *Brahman*?

The Upaniṣadic answer to these questions constitutes the central and the most profound insight and teaching of the *ṛṣis* (the Vedic sages and seers). *Brahman,* the timeless and enduring reality amidst and behind the unceasingly changing external world, although infinite and eternal, lacks spirituality. On the other hand, *ātman,* the eternal and abiding reality amidst and behind the shifting and changing internal world, although spiritual, lacks infinitude. That is, there is no self-contradiction in thinking that the *infinite Brahman* is a purely material (meaning, "devoid of consciousness," *jaḍa*) reality; nor is it self-contradictory to think that *ātman* is a finite spiritual reality. But now the sages noticed that by identifying *Brahman* and *ātman,* they could in one stroke render *ātman* spirit infinite and *Brahman* infinite spirit. Thus the *ṛṣi*s declared that *ātman* and *Brahman* do not refer to two numerically distinguishable realities, but are two different labels for one and the same timeless and hence eternal and immortal reality whose manifestations are the changing worlds of phenomena, external as well as internal. (An important comment before we move on: the above is not to be construed as saying that the Upaniṣadic sages arrived at their declaration that *Brahman* and *ātman* are non-different through a cerebral — sensory-mental — process. Quite to the contrary, they first realized the profound truth through their own — direct, existential, and hence authentic — non-dual mystical experience, transcending the senses and intellect. *We* are trying to understand how the *ṛṣis* subsequently came to articulate their insights and experiences — that is, how they intellectually formulated and communicated their knowledge and wisdom; this account is therefore our reconstruction.)

Here is reached the pinnacle of the Upaniṣadic wisdom: *tat kvam asi* (That thou art, *Kena* I), *ayam ātmā Brahma* (This Self is Brahman, *Bṛhadāraṇyaka* I.iv.10), and *prajñānam Brahma* (Pure consciousness is Brahman, *Bṛhadāraṇyaka* II.5). These declarations are known as *mahāvākyas*, meaning great pronouncements. Further,

> What is within us is also without. What is without is also within. He who sees difference between what is within and what is without goes evermore from death to death.
>
> — *Aitareya* III.i.3

> The self who understands all, who knows all, and whose glory is manifested in the universe, lives within the shrine of the heart, the city of *Brahman*. — *Kaṭha* II.iv.10

> That which is the subtle essence — in that have all beings their existence. That is the truth. That is the Self. And that, O Śvetaketu, That art Thou. — *Chāndogya* VI.x.3

> Formless is he, though inhabiting form. In the midst of the fleeting he abides forever. All-pervading and supreme is the Self. The wise, knowing him in his true nature, transcend all grief. — *Kaṭha* I.ii.22

Knowledge and Freedom (Mokṣa)

The Upaniṣads distinguish between two kinds of knowledge: the lower knowledge (*aparā vidyā*) and the higher knowledge (*parā vidyā*). The former is the product of the senses and intellect and is accordingly limited to the finite, objective world of change and impermanence. On the other hand, the higher knowledge is that by which the infinite and imperishable *Brahman* is attained:

> There are two kinds of knowledge, the higher and the lower. The lower is knowledge of the Vedas (the *Ṛg*, the *Sāma*, the *Yajur*, and the *Atharva*), and also of phonetics, ceremonials, grammar, etymology, metre and astronomy. The higher knowledge is of that by which one knows the changeless Reality. By this is fully revealed to the wise that which transcends the senses, which is uncaused, which is undefinable, which has neither eyes nor ears, neither hands nor feet, which is all-pervading, subtler than the subtlest — the everlasting, the source of all. — *Muṇḍaka* I.i.4-6

The higher knowledge, unlike the lower, is non-perceptual, non-conceptual, and intuitive. It is direct and immediate and is attained only by those who have stilled their senses and mind. Further, the higher knowledge is neither objective nor subjective, for it transcends all three categories of empirical experience, namely, the knower, the known, and the act of knowing. Neither the performance of rituals and sacrifices nor the singing of the hymns nor the chanting of the *mantra*s can bring one the higher knowledge:

> The Self is not known through the study of scriptures, nor through subtlety of the intellect, nor through much learning. But by him who longs for him is he known. Verily unto him does the Self reveal his true being. — *Kaṭha* I.ii.23

It is truly remarkable that the *ṛṣi*s declare even the Vedas to be lower knowledge; and to the best of my knowledge and belief, there is no other tradition which so regards its own sacred writings and scriptures. The reason for such a declaration on the part of the *ṛṣi*s must be clear: the Vedas are couched in language, hence are a product of percepts and concepts, thereby lacking the power to capture and reveal *Brahman* which transcends the senses and intellect. It is abundantly clear from the passage quoted above that the Upaniṣadic sages regard all rational-scientific knowledge as lower knowledge; and it needs to be emphasized here that the term "lower knowledge" is not intended to belittle, dis-value, denigrate, and reject rational-scientific knowledge. Rather, it is to call attention to the fact that rational-scientific knowledge is the product of the operation of the senses and mind — of percepts and concepts — valid and reliable in its own proper domain.

Mokṣa, freedom from ignorance and bondage, is not a postmortem state, a state to be looked forward to after death; rather, it is to be attained *here and now,* in this life. He who attains the knowledge of *Brahman* while still in bodily existence is the *jīvanmukta* (the living-free). He has conquered ignorance and delusion once and for all. Gone is he beyond birth and death. He has attained immortality. At his death, the *jīvanmukta* attains *kaivalya,* total and absolute freedom:

> Having fully ascertained and realized the truth of Vedānta, having established themselves in purity of conduct by following the yoga of renunciation, these great ones attain to immortality in this very life. — *Muṇḍaka* III.ii.6

It should be emphasized in the context of the Upaniṣads that immortality is not to be understood as endless existence in some unknown, distant corner of the cosmos, but as the state of consciousness in which one gains insight into the very ground of all existence. To attain such consciousness is to attain immortality. Immortality is *saccidānanda* (*sat* = pure being, *cit* = pure consciousness, *ānanda* = pure bliss).

As the path to the realization of *Brahman* (*ātman*), the Upaniṣads recommend the fourfold discipline:

(1) cultivation of moral purity as well as the disposition and will to seek the liberating knowledge, namely, the knowledge of *Brahman,* of *ātman;*

(2) listening attentively to a teacher (*guru,* the liberated human being) as he or she expounds the Upaniṣadic truths;

(3) reflecting upon the truths thus heard; and

(4) meditation.

> To many it is not given to hear of the Self. Many, though they hear of it, do not understand it. Wonderful is he who speaks of it; intelligent is he who learns of it. Blessed is he who, taught by a good teacher, is able to understand it. — *Kaṭha* I.ii.7

> The truth of the Self cannot be fully understood when taught by an ignorant man, for opinions regarding it, not founded on knowledge, vary one from another. Subtler than the subtlest is this Self, and beyond all logic. Taught by a teacher who knows the Self and *Brahman* as one, a man leaves vain theory behind and attains to truth. — *Kaṭha* I.ii.8

> Words cannot reveal him. Mind is unable to reach him. The eyes do not see him. How then can he be comprehended save when taught by those seers who indeed have known him? — *Kaṭha* II.vi.12

> Affix to the Upaniṣad, the bow incomparable, the sharp arrow of devotional worship; then, with mind absorbed and heart melted in love, draw the arrow and hit the mark, the Imperishable *Brahman. Oṁ* is the bow, the arrow is the individual being, and *Brahman* is the target. With a tranquil heart, take aim. Lose thyself in him, even as the arrow is lost in the target. In him are woven heaven, earth, and sky, together with the mind and all the senses. Know him, the Self alone. Give up vain talk. He is the bridge of immortality. Within the lotus of the heart he dwells, where, like the spokes of a wheel, the nerves meet. Meditate on him as *oṁ*. Easily mayest thou cross the sea of darkness. — *Muṇḍaka* II.ii.3-6

Such, then, is the sublime non-dualism of the Upaniṣadic teaching of the non-difference of *ātman* and *Brahman*. The human being's state of bondage and unfreedom is due to ignorance of her or his true being. By destroying this primordial ignorance, one comes to know oneself as the eternal and infinite *Brahman*.

Nothing could be a more fitting conclusion to this exposition of the central teachings of the Upaniṣads than the following delightful fable, told by the great seer Sri Ramakrishna:

> A lioness in search of prey came upon a flock of sheep, and as she jumped at one of them, she gave birth to a cub and died on the spot. The young lion was brought up in the flock, ate grass and bleated like a sheep, and it never knew that it was a lion. One day a lion came across this flock and was astonished to see in it a huge lion eating grass and bleating like a sheep. At his sight the flock fled and the lion-sheep with them. But the lion watched his opportunity and found the lion-sheep asleep. He woke him up and said, "You are a lion." The other said, "No," and began to bleat like a sheep. But the stranger lion took him to a lake and asked him to look in the water at his own image and see if it did not resemble him, the stranger lion. He looked and acknowledged that it did. Then the stranger lion began to roar and asked him to do the same. The lion-sheep tried his voice and was soon roaring as grandly as the other. And he was a sheep no longer.
>
> — *The Complete Works of Swami Vivekananda,* Mayaavati: Advaita Ashrama, 1950, vol. 1, pp. 324-25

In truth, everyone of us is *Brahman,* but in our ignorance we think that we are finite, perishable beings. The Upaniṣads exhort us to cut through the cloud of ignorance and discover ourselves to be *Brahman,* infinite, eternal, and immortal.

2

Clarification and Discussion

THE main purpose of this chapter is to systematically examine and clarify the central Upaniṣadic concepts and declarations, which have been textually documented in the last chapter. I am not interested here in defending any particular school of Vedānta, identified by a certain interpretation of the Upaniṣads. Rather, I wish to present here my own understanding of the teaching of thoroughgoing and uncompromising non-dualism of the Upaniṣads, an understanding that is the result of more than fifty years of study and practice. I do, however, acknowledge that non-dualism, as systematized and formulated by Śaṅkara (seventh-eighth centuries CE), the great scholar, poet, mystic, and founder of the school of Advaita Vedānta (Non-dualistic Vedānta), is most faithful to the Upaniṣadic texts themselves. This does not, however, mean that my prime concern here is to discuss Śaṅkara's Advaita Vedānta. It only means that my own explication of the non-dualism of the Upaniṣads is in full accord with Śaṅkara's Advaita Vedānta. For this reason, wherever and whenever appropriate and necessary, I shall freely draw upon Śaṅkara's Advaita Vedānta.

We have pointed out earlier that the Upaniṣads are not systematic philosophical treatises, but are primarily the record of the utterances of the sages concerning their intuitive insights into and direct experience of ultimate reality. Consequently, one encounters in the Upaniṣads apparently inconsistent statements, different degrees of emphasis on the same idea at different times, and sometimes seemingly irrelevant digressions. Further, the terse and aphoristic style of the Upaniṣads and the esoteric nature of the subject of their teachings make it difficult to grasp the ideas. It is therefore not surprising that in course of time different people understood the Upaniṣads in different ways and accordingly a need for systematizing the fundamental ideas of the Upaniṣads was keenly felt. The earliest attempt to systematically present the Upaniṣadic thought was the celebrated *Brahmasūtras* (also known as *Vedāntasūtras* and *Śārīraka-sūtras*) of Bādarāyaṇa, which is justly regarded as the cornerstone of all Vedāntic thought. The *Brahmasūtras* has been the source of inspiration for all Vedāntic thinkers, great and small alike. It should be pointed out, however, that the *Brahmasūtras* itself is couched in brief and compact statements, which lend themselves to a variety of meanings and interpretations. For this reason, subsequent Vedāntic thinkers wrote elaborate commentaries, each interpreting the *Brahmasūtras* and the Upaniṣads in their own way. In this manner there arose various schools of Vedānta, of which the most important are Śaṅkara's Advaita Vedānta (non-dualistic Vedānta), Rāmānuja's Viśiṣṭādvaita Vedānta (qualified non-dualistic Vedānta), and Madhva's Dvaita Vedānta (dualistic Vedānta). Of these three, Śaṅkara's Advaita Vedānta is the most prominent and influential. Next in influence is Rāmānuja's Viśiṣṭādvaita Vedānta, and the least prominent and influential is Madhva's Dvaita Vedānta. The greatness of Advaita Vedānta lies in the fact that it can easily accommodate within itself the other two schools of Vedānta, whereas the latter two lack the breadth, depth, and scope to accommodate Advaita Vedānta. I shall now turn to a clarification of *Brahman, ātman,* and the claim of their non-difference.

Brahman is unborn, uncreated, undying, eternal, and immortal. *Brahman* is formless and nameless and is therefore imperceivable, inconceivable, and hence indescribable and inexpressible. *Brahman* is neither a he nor a she, but That. *Brahman* is that whose varieties of manifestations are the worlds of phenomena. What is a phenomenon? Here is the definition: a phenomenon is anything that is, or can in principle be, an object of consciousness. All phenomena exist in time, although some phenomena also exist in space. Thus, tables, tigers, stars, galaxies, people, etc. exist in both space and time. That is, we can assign them both spatial and temporal locations (x, y, z, t). In sharp contrast, thoughts, feelings, emotions, mental images — including dreams — exist only in time and cannot be assigned any spatial locations. Time is thus the primary co-ordinate of all phenomenal existence; that is, whatever exists or can exist as a phenomenon necessarily exists in time. To exist in time is to have a beginning and an end — arising and passing away — and hence is to be subject to change. All phenomena, therefore, are subject to change. In other words, every phenomenon is ineluctably subject to birth and death. That *Brahman* is unborn, uncreated, and undying, then, means that *Brahman* is *not* a phenomenon. That is precisely the reason why *Brahman* cannot be perceived by the senses or conceived of by the mind. Whatever the senses and mind can capture is therefore a phenomenon, an object of consciousness.

But what does it mean to say that the worlds of phenomena are the varieties of manifestation of *Brahman*? In order to clarify this point, consider a gold necklace. One can take the necklace to a goldsmith, have it melted down and made into, say, a bracelet. The Upaniṣadic sage's question here is, "What has changed?" And he goes on to tell us that the change is only in form and hence name; what was hitherto called a "necklace" is now called a "bracelet." The stuff of which they are made did not undergo any *real* change, "real change" being understood as one through which something becomes something else, *radically* different from itself, by losing its essential being and nature. In the above analogical illustration, gold, of which the necklace and the bracelet are merely manifestations, did not undergo any real change, by becoming something other than gold; it still is the *same* gold, the stuff of which the necklace as well as the bracelet is made — their very being, their very *existence.* Just as the same, unchanging gold appears as a necklace at one time and a bracelet at another, so also *Brahman,* of which all existents — phenomena — are constituted, undergoes no *real* change in manifesting Itself as the variety and multiplicity of phenomena and remains the same. *Brahman* is That of which all phenomena — things, objects of consciousness in general — are made. *Brahman* is capable of manifesting Itself as various phenomena, precisely because *Brahman* is not Itself a phenomenon, a thing, an object of consciousness. Just as clay can be made into cups, saucers, jars, and so on and still remains as clay even after the cups, saucers, jars, and so on, are destroyed, say, by being beaten with a hammer, so also *Brahman* persists even when all phenomena — all of Its manifestations — disappear. Likewise, just as the cups, saucers, jars, and so on have no existence apart from the clay, so also phenomena have no existence apart from *Brahman.* In other words, phenomena depend for their existence on *Brahman,* just as cups, saucers, jars, and so on depend for their existence on clay. Just as clay does not depend for its existence on the existence of cups, saucers, jars, and so on, so also *Brahman* does not depend for Its existence on phenomena. In short, *Brahman* is *self-existent,* the *only self-existent.* Every phenomenon is a dependent existent, each phenomenon depending upon other phenomena and all phenomena depending upon *Brahman.* Phenomena come into being and pass away, whereas *Brahman* never *comes* into being and *passes* away. *Brahman* always was, is, and will be. In short, whereas all phenomena are time-bound, *Brahman* transcends time. Thus there are two ways of understanding *Brahman*: *Brahman* as immanent and *Brahman* as transcendent. *Brahman* is immanent in the sense that all phenomena are but manifestations of *Brahman;* and *Brahman* is transcendent in the sense that that of which all phenomena are manifestations is not Itself a manifestation — a phenomenon — and therefore transcends both space and time and cannot be captured by the senses and the mind. Try to visualize — picture — transcendent *Brahman;* you will see that *Brahman* cannot be visualized or pictured, because whatever can be visualized or pictured is always, ineluctably, a phenomenon, an object, a time-bound existent.

What are our best physicists busy with? They are trying to find out *that* of which all things are made. The Upaniṣadic sage will tell the physicists that they should continue their researches and find out interesting things about subtler and subtler *phenomena* but that they will never be able to capture in their theories and high-energy accelerators *that* of which all things are made. The reason for this is that whatever one can grasp in theories and high-energy accelerators is always, inevitably, a phenomenon, an object; and one can always ask, "what is that made of?" Put another way, all phenomena, being non-self-existents, are composite, made up of parts; in keen contrast, transcendent *Brahman,* being self-existent and formless, is not a phenomenon and is therefore impartite, not made up of parts (for if *Brahman* were made up of parts, the parts will be fundamental and ultimate, not *Brahman).* The point of all these observations, then, is that *Brahman* as transcendent cannot be grasped by the senses and intellect.

Another way of understanding *Brahman* is as follows: Look around the room, you will see so many phenomena, lamps, books, people, the coffeepot, cups, milk, sugar, an ant crawling by the wall, and so on. These phenomena clearly differ from each other in so many ways, but what is it they all have in common? What they all unmistakably have in common is the fact of *existence.* This existence is *Brahman.* Hence the Upaniṣadic declaration: Whatever exists (or can in principle exist) is *Brahman. Brahman* is existence (*sat*). *Sat,* existence, can never become non-existence (*asat*). What is more, non-existence (*asat*) can never become existence (*sat*). Nothing other than *Brahman* can exist; that is, *Brahman* is that beside which nothing exists (or can exist). Hence *Brahman* is that without a second (*advitīyam*). One can, then, in the light of all these considerations, express the Upaniṣadic insight into *Brahman* as the Principle of Conservation of Existence (*sat*).

What, then, are the worlds of phenomena — objects, physical

as well as mental and emotional, external as well as internal? They are all varieties of manifestations of *Brahman,* the very source of *all* existence. Thus, when you see, for example, the bird flying over, you should see it and understand it as a manifestation of *Brahman,* a bearer and revealer of the mystery of *Brahman* in its own unique way.

Brahman is not to be understood as the creator of the universe. Quite to the contrary, *Brahman is* the universe. But since *Brahman* is transcendent, *Brahman* is not exhausted by the universe. *Brahman* is more than and excels the universe at any given time, for things (phenomena) which did not exist before come into being, and they cannot, in principle, come out of non-existence. Rather, whatever comes into existence is but a manifestation of the immeasurable, illimitable, formless *Brahman,* Existence (*sat*); remember, *asat* (non-existence) can never become *sat* (existence)? Only *sat,* Existence (*Brahman*), can *manifest* Itself as phenomena, which surely are existence. Existence cannot come from non-existence, but only from Existence, *Brahman.*

The world of phenomena, of our senses and intellect, *is Brahman;* it is *manifest Brahman;* it has no existence apart from *Brahman.* Thus sacredness and holiness are not the exclusive properties of some being hiding in a cosmic closet; rather, the entire world, being none other than the variety and multiplicity of manifestations of *Brahman,* is through and through sacred and holy. In this manner, whosoever understands this profound teaching of the Upaniṣadic sages comes to see the world in a radically different way, as *Brahman* Itself.

According to the Western religious traditions, God created the world out of nothing — *creatio ex nihilo.* The Upaniṣadic sage will say that such a view is not rational; for, if prior to the creation of the world, only God existed and nothing else, it is only rational to understand the statement "God created the world" as meaning that God *became* the world, for nothing can be created out of nothing — *asat* cannot become *sat* — non-existence cannot, in principle, become existence. And God is not exhausted by his creation, the world. To think that God created the world out of nothing, is to think of God as a cheap stage-magician who, by sleight of hand, produces something out of nothing, say, a bird out of an empty hat. According to the Upaniṣads, *Brahman* is not the creator of the world; rather *Brahman is* the world and more than the world. This way of understanding is in full accord with the highest standards of rationality and still does full justice to the idea that God created the world.

Let me now clarify the teaching that *Brahman* is at once immanent and transcendent. Consider for example, two phenomena, say a tree and a bird, respectively denoted by P1 and P2. According to the Upaniṣads, P1 = *Brahman* and P2 = *Brahman,* and it logically follows then that P1 = P2. But we know that P1 is not identical to P2, the tree is not identical to the bird. Thus there seems to be a contradiction. How does the Upaniṣadic sage explain this? He will tell us that as *phenomena* the tree and the bird are different; but they are identical in the sense that they are two different manifestations of one and the same reality, just as the necklace and the bracelet are two different manifestations of one and the same reality, namely, gold. The tree and the bird differ only in name and form, but that of which they are manifestations is one and the same, the transcendent *Brahman.* Understood in this manner, there is no contradiction, which only arises out of one's failure to distinguish between *Brahman* as immanent and *Brahman* as transcendent.

Why do we need names? What purpose is served by names? We need names in order to distinguish one form from another, one phenomenon from another. Thus when one says, this is a tree and that is a bird, one is distinguishing the tree-form from the bird-form. It logically follows then that where there are no forms there cannot be any names, either. Since the transcendent *Brahman* is formless, It is also nameless. This is the meaning of the Upaniṣadic declaration that *Brahman* is formless and nameless. Someone might think that *Brahman* is a name and therefore there seems to be a contradiction in the Upaniṣadic teaching that *Brahman* is nameless. *Brahman* is *not* a name; rather, it is merely a symbol the *ṛṣis* employ in order to facilitate discourse and communication. One is therefore free to use any symbol one wishes without making any difference to the insight and its expression. Does it really make any difference to the teaching if one uses "Nahbram" instead of *Brahman*? It makes absolutely no difference.

Nothing can be positively said of *Brahman,* the transcendent *Brahman;* one can only say, *Brahman* is not this, not that, and so on. What does this mean? Nothing can be positively said of the transcendent *Brahman,* because, by not being a phenomenon, an object alongside other objects, transcendent *Brahman* has neither properties nor relations. Only phenomena — objects — can have properties and relations. Further, since nothing other than *Brahman* can exist, there can be nothing to which *Brahman* can be related. A word about properties. Consider the sentence, "This apple is red." Through this sentence, one is saying that a particular thing — this apple — has the property of redness. But since transcendent *Brahman* is not a thing, It cannot have any properties. The above sentence is possible only by distinguishing between things and properties, and no distinctions are possible in regard to transcendent *Brahman,* since It is formless and hence not a thing.

One can, however, point to *any* phenomenon — any object — and say it is *Brahman,* without implying that other phenomena are not *Brahman;* the reason for this is that *all* phenomena are *Brahman,* in the sense that all phenomena are *manifestations* of *Brahman.* One can only point to a phenomenon and describe it, but one can never point to *that,* the transcendent *Brahman,* of which the phenomenon is but one manifestation, and describe It. Thus the declaration that all phenomena are *Brahman* means that the very being — existence — of any and all phenomena is the transcendent *Brahman, Sat* — Existence.

Imagine someone taking out a bucket of water and a glass

of water from the ocean. The water in the bucket is of the form of the bucket and the water in the glass is of the form of the glass. There is more water in the bucket than in the glass, but there is absolutely no difference in the essence and existence between the water in the bucket and the water in the glass. Analysis reveals no difference at all between the water in the bucket and the water in the glass. Further, when one throws back the bucket of water and the glass of water into the ocean, they no longer can be identified as the water which was in the bucket and the water which was in the glass. What does this all mean? It means that differences in form and name have no bearing at all on the oneness of essence and existence. All phenomena, irrespective of their forms and names, are of the same essence and existence, the transcendent *Brahman*.

One might wonder as to why in our explication of *Brahman* we constantly employ analogies and metaphors. The reason for this must be obvious: Since *Brahman* transcends the senses and intellect and defies any and all descriptions, we have no other way of clarifying the insight into *Brahman* than through analogical and metaphorical discourse. The analogies and metaphors do not constitute arguments; and arguments, being the product of the senses and the mind, cannot capture *Brahman* and hence are of no avail here. Nevertheless, the analogies and metaphors, when clearly grasped, serve to awaken our intuition and thereby orient us to the quest for *Brahman*. The Upaniṣadic sages are primarily concerned with awakening our intuition and therefore they freely employ whatever mode of discourse best serves this purpose.

If we ask the physicists what drives their inquiries into finding out *that* of which all things are made, what can they say in reply? They can only reply by saying that it is their hunch — intuitive feeling — that motivates and drives their inquiries. Thus the Upaniṣadic teaching of *Brahman* is in full accord and harmony with the intuition underlying the scientific quest for *that* of which all things are made. However, one should bear in mind that *that* cannot, in principle, be captured in theories and high-energy accelerators. Are we then to despair and give up scientific inquiry? Certainly not; scientific inquiry, being a product of the senses and the mind, although cannot reveal the transcendent *Brahman,* surely enlarges and deepens our knowledge and understanding of increasingly subtle varieties of phenomena. Thus we should continue our scientific researches, without the illusion that one day they will reveal to us the transcendent *Brahman.* Transcendent *Brahman* is to be realized by other means, which we shall later discuss. The main point I wish to make here is that there is absolutely no incompatibility — no opposition, no contradiction — between conducting scientific inquiry and being engaged in the quest for transcendent *Brahman.* In other words, contrary to the widespread but uncritical view, one and the same person can be a rational-scientific thinker and a mystic. In short, mystical pursuit is not to be construed as requiring the abandonment and rejection of rational-scientific inquiries. Rational-scientific pursuits are concerned with knowledge and understanding of phenomena — *manifestations* of the transcendent *Brahman* — whereas the mystical pursuit is concerned with knowledge of the transcendent *Brahman* Itself. Rational-scientific knowledge is gathered through the operation of the senses and intellect, whereas knowledge of the transcendent *Brahman* requires the transcending of the senses and intellect.

The Upaniṣadic sages sometimes talk about *Brahman* as power. The power displayed in the lightning and thunder and the power displayed in the winking of the eyes and the movements of the mind are one and the same power. Whatever exists is power. Every manifestation of *Brahman* is power. Thus a stone is a manifestation of power. How so? Our best science tells us, in full agreement with the proclamation of the *ṛṣis,* that when the stone is analyzed you will discover it to be made up of varieties of particles — molecules, atoms, electrons, nucleons — in a state of incessant motion. Motion is power, dynamism. There is no such thing as power that is not dynamism, actual or potential. In our study of the constitution of the so-called matter, we arrive at a point where we can only *describe* motion, whose causes elude us. That motion is power. This is the meaning of the sage's teaching that *Brahman* is power. All manifestations of *Brahman* are power. A word of caution: One should not hereby think that the transcendent *Brahman* is power; rather, it means that every *manifestation* of the transcendent *Brahman* is power. One can easily think of particular forms of power, such as gravitational, electric, electromagnetic, sonic, nuclear, and so on, but one cannot, in principle, think and visualize power *qua* power, power as such. That power is *Brahman.* This is the closest that we can come to intellectually understanding the *ṛṣi*'s teaching that *Brahman* is power.

To take another example, have you ever thought about the hamburger you just bought and consumed? What exactly is the hamburger? What is it made of? One will say that someone slaughtered a cow or bull and its meat is the hamburger. But where did the meat come from? How did it come about? One will say that the cow ate grass and grain. But how did the grass and grain come about? One will again answer by saying that the grass and grain came about through the interactions of the seeds, soil, water, minerals, and sunshine. But how did these things come about? The inquiry goes on to the sun, the galaxies, and beyond. What all this means is that the hamburger that you bought and ate is a packet of power; the hamburger is an intersection of power-lines emanating from different parts of the cosmos. How far one wants to take the analysis depends upon one's purposes. But it is clear that the entire cosmos is nothing but power, and that power is *Brahman.* And do not forget that you are yourself a packet of power, a manifestation of the transcendent *Brahman.* Hence the sage's teaching, "I am *Brahman.*" Your very being, very existence, is none other than the transcendent *Brahman, sat,* besides which nothing can exist.

In this connection, it is important to clarify the Upaniṣadic teaching that *Brahman* is non-dual. *Brahman* is non-dual in two senses: 1. Nothing other than *Brahman* can exist, and 2. *Brahman* is impartite — not made up of parts. That is, there can be no duality either within or without *Brahman*. Only phenomena — objects, manifestations of *Brahman* — are partite, have parts, and there are many objects. Some scholars refer to the Upaniṣadic teaching as monism, meaning a single reality. This is not quite correct, for "one" refers to number which can only be properly applied with respect to phenomena — objects — whereas the transcendent *Brahman*, not being an object, cannot be referred to as "one." For this reason, it is most appropriately and correctly referred to, by the *ṛṣi*s, as "non-dual," meaning "not-many." One might now object by saying, "doesn't not many" imply "one"?" Yes, "not many," understood as pertaining to the world of phenomena — objects, plurality, variety and multiplicity — certainly implies "one," but that is to entirely miss the point of the *ṛṣi*'s message. The *ṛṣi*'s teaching is that number cannot properly be applied to the transcendent *Brahman*, Which is *not* a *thing*, and hence it is improper and misleading to refer to It as "one." "Not many" means "not a thing," because "many" goes with things, the domain of plurality. You can properly say, "there are many things," only when the word "thing" has meaning and reference; but you can never say, "there is just one *Brahman*" (just as you can say that there is just one coffee cup in this room), because *Brahman* is *not a thing*, and therefore it is best to say, "*Brahman* is non-dual (not-many)." That is exactly the Upaniṣadic sages' teaching. Yes, many mystics, Eastern and Western, referred to ultimate reality as "the one," for example, Plotinus, the great mystic, who was the fountainhead of Western mysticism, including the Christian. This observation is not to be construed as saying that Plotinus and others who proclaimed ultimate reality as "the one" are mistaken and did not realize *Brahman;* rather, the point is that they did not *express* their insight into the non-dual reality most precisely — yes, from a linguistic point of view — at once preserving its intuitive and intellectual basis. The *ṛṣi*s are at once intuitively extraordinary and intellectually most profound and subtle.

I come now to a clarification of *ātman*. *Ātman*, like *Brahman*, is unborn, uncreated, undying, eternal, and immortal. Further, like *Brahman*, *ātman*, transcending the senses and intellect, is imperceivable, inconceivable, and inexpressible. *Ātman* is not to be confused with the empirical ego — *jīva*. When one uses the words "I" and "me," they refer to the empirical ego. Thus, when one says, "I am fat," one is referring to the body; and when one says, "I am depressed," one is referring to the mind. *Jīva*, the empirical ego, then, is best understood as the psycho-physiological complex, constituted through and through of phenomenal strands. This means that, like every other phenomenon, the empirical ego is a time-bound existent, that is, it is subject to change and therefore arises and passes away. It is the empirical ego that is studied in psychological laboratories. The empirical ego can be visualized, pictured, and described. In keen contrast, *ātman* is pure, objectless consciousness, and is therefore formless and nameless, hence cannot be perceived by the senses and the mind. No one can visualize and picture *ātman*. Try as you may, to visualize and picture pure consciousness, and you will see the point. Have you ever received a telephone call from a friend asking you, "How is your consciousness this morning? Is it round and red? Or is it yellow and elliptical?" How then does one know that there is *ātman*? The answer is surprisingly simple and straightforward: It is not given to anyone to be able to deny consciousness. Have you ever received a telephone call from a friend saying, "John, I don't know what is happening to me, I am not conscious now?" Certainly not; for, in order to be able to deny anything, consciousness is necessary. That consciousness, imperceivable and inconceivable and yet in principle undeniable, is *ātman*. *Ātman* is pure consciousness.

Is the consciousness, *qua* consciousness (consciousness as such) of one human being distinguishable from the consciousness of another human being? The Upaniṣadic answer to this question is clearly in the negative; only phenomena, objects, can be distinguished from each other, and consciousness cannot be so distinguished. The reason for this is that consciousness, not being a phenomenon — an object — bears no marks. We distinguish one object from another by the marks they bear, and where there are no marks, one cannot distinguish. This means that consciousness — *ātman* — is never plural. It is a grave error to talk of *ātmans*, for *ātman*, like *Brahman*, is non-dual. Thus, that there are twenty people in a room does not mean that there are twenty consciousness*es* in the room; rather it means that there are twenty *conscious beings* in the room, each distinguishable from another by its spatial location. Put otherwise, there are twenty different *manifestations* of consciousness in the room. *Ātman* is always non-dual. There simply cannot be *ātmans*.

Consider the following: A certain person, John, says at a certain time, "I'm an engineer, a husband, and a republican." You run into him a few years later in an airport lounge and hear him saying, "I'm a professional boxer, I'm divorced, and I'm no longer a republican but a committed democrat." The Upaniṣadic *ṛṣi*'s observation and question here are: We clearly notice several differences among the various things John was and now is; but we also notice the "I am" in everyone of these sentences. The question is, "Who or what is the *I am* that invariably and unavoidably appears in these sentences?" The *ṛṣi*'s exhortation is to discover the answer to this question. This discovery is the coming to know one's true being, whose *appearances* are the everchanging empirical ego and the variety of states of its being. Śrī Ramaṇa Maharṣı, the great Indian mystic, widely known and highly revered and admired around the world, exhorted everyone, in quest of liberating knowledge and wisdom, to strive to answer the question, "Who am I?" The "I," in its true being, is the unborn, uncreated, undying, and therefore eternal and immortal *ātman*.

In order to further drive the point home, consider the following: A certain person, James, says, "I'm a teacher, a father, and a musician," and another person, Tom, says, "I'm a policeman, a bachelor, and breeder of dogs." Notice that there is the "I am" in both the sentences, although they were uttered by two different persons. What does this "I am" refer to? The "I am," according to the Upaniṣadic sages, refers to *ātman,* pure consciousness, which remains the same, irrespective of any and all circumstances. What is more, the "I am" of John's utterance and the "I am" of Tom's utterance are *numerically indistinguishable.* That is, differences are only to be found among the *jīvas* — the empirical egos — but never with regard to the "I am." The "I am" refers to the non-dual *ātman,* pure consciousness, no matter who the speaker. Different persons are different appearances — manifestations, embodiments — of the non-dual *ātman.*

What about non-human animals? Is the consciousness of, say a cat, numerically distinguishable from the consciousness of a human being? The Upaniṣadic answer is again a definite "No." The reason for this is that consciousness as such bears no marks, by which distinctions are made. This means that the consciousness of a cat cannot be distinguished from the consciousness of a human being or of any other kind of being. One can only distinguish between objects of consciousness. Thus, for example, the concept of a Euclidean triangle can never be an object of consciousness of a cat. The reason for the difference between the ranges and kinds of objects a cat can be conscious of and those the human being can be conscious of is traceable to differences between the psycho-physiological constitutions of a cat and a human being — that is, to differences in the constitutions of the *jīvas*. The upshot of these observations is that *ātman,* pure consciousness, can never be in plural, but always non-dual.

Let it be emphasized that even amnesiacs and schizophrenics cannot be without the "I." Thus when you ask an amnesiac, lost somewhere in a town, "What's your name and where do you live?" he tells you, "*I* don't know"; and we are familiar with the fact that schizophrenics proclaim, "*I*'m Napoleon," "*I*'m Jesus," and so on. The point here is that there is the "*I*" in these proclamations, referring to *ātman,* pure consciousness, despite loss of memory and split personality.

One can get rid of everything, but consciousness cannot be gotten rid of, because getting rid of anything requires consciousness.

What precisely, then, is the relation between *ātman* and *jīva* — the empirical ego? According to the Upaniṣadic sages, *jīva* is an *appearance* of *ātman,* under the limiting conditions (*upādhi*), namely, the psycho-physiological complex. Thus consider a person, John X, who is a theatrical actor: John plays one day the role of Alexander, another day that of Caesar, yet another day of Napoleon. No matter how many times one sees John's performances, one does not come to know John, the actor himself. The Alexander, Caesar, Napoleon, and so on one sees on the stage are the *appearances* of John. One never comes to know John himself, because one has never seen John apart from his appearances. Just so, one never comes to know the *ātman,* by only seeing the variety of appearances — *jīva* — of the *ātman.* The question now is, "Do the Alexander, Caesar, and Napoleon we see on the stage have any existence apart from — independently of — John the actor?" The answer clearly is in the negative. They have absolutely no existence of their own, for they are merely the appearances of the same John X. The Alexander, Caesar, and Napoleon we see on the stage appear, disappear, and reappear, but John the actor himself persists even when he is not performing in the theatre. Just so, *ātman,* the "I am," persists, even though the *jīva* appears, disappears, and re-appears. (Remember the example earlier of someone who described himself as an engineer and husband at one time and as a professional boxer and divorced at a later time.)

Let us now give another illustration to further clarify the point. Consider space. We talk about the space in the jar, the space in the box, the space in the wallet, and so on. Does this mean that there are so many numerically distinguishable spaces? Certainly not. There is just unitary space, and "space in the jar" means not another space, but rather space under the limiting conditions (*upādhi*), namely the jar; and even when the jar is broken and destroyed, the space remains the same. Just so, *ātman* is non-dual, and its appearances under varying limiting conditions of psycho-physiological complexes are the *jīva*(s). It should be abundantly clear by now that the *jīva* is an *appearance* of the *ātman* and has absolutely no existence apart from — independently of — the *ātman. Jīva* is thus a phenomenon, an *object* of consciousness, which can be assigned spatial and temporal coordinates, whereas the *ātman,* like *Brahman,* is transcendent, imperceivable, inconceivable, indescribable, and inexpressible.

There are philosophers who refer to consciousness as a "phenomenon." There are even books bearing titles such as "The *structure* of consciousness." These philosophers are wholly mistaken and do not have even the faintest idea as to what consciousness is. If consciousness is a *phenomenon,* consciousness should appear as an *object;* have you ever experienced consciousness as an object? Further, if consciousness appears as a phenomenon — an object — to whom does it appear? The Upaniṣadic sage will tell us that consciousness *never* appears as an object, a phenomenon. Quite to the contrary, consciousness makes it possible for there to be any appearances at all. It is the matrix in which objects appear, itself not being an object. Only objects can have structures, and since consciousness is not an object, alongside other objects, it does not have any structure. Consciousness, *ātman,* like *Brahman,* is impartite. To have structure, is to be partite, and since consciousness is impartite, it cannot have any structure. Thus those who think that consciousness is a phenomenon — an object — and has a structure are, according to the Upaniṣadic seers, among the most ignorant.

In order to further substantiate his teaching, the *ṛṣi* requires us to examine the following: You are at time t1 conscious of object 01, a picture on the wall, and at time t2 of object 02, a glass of water on the table, and at time t3 of object 03, the letter from a friend you just received in the mail. You certainly notice differences among the three objects of consciousness, but the question is, "Do you also notice any difference in consciousness as such at t1, t2, and t3?" The answer is clearly in the negative. You do not notice any change in consciousness. Changes can only be among objects of consciousness and never in consciousness itself, and that selfsame consciousness is the *ātman.* Why didn't you notice any change in consciousness? Answer: Consciousness is not an object, a phenomenon. Change implies time, and since consciousness, *ātman,* transcends time, no changes can be observed in *ātman.*

The above analysis clearly shows that *ātman,* like *Brahman,* is formless, nameless, and transcends the senses and intellect, and therefore, is indescribable and inexpressible. Just as no one can deny *Brahman* (Existence), since there are phenomena — objects of consciousness — so also no one can deny *ātman,* since no one can say, "I am not conscious."

One might now ask, "Are there, then, according to the Upaniṣadic sage, two ultimate realities, *Brahman,* whose varieties of manifestation are the external world of phenomena on the one hand, and *ātman,* whose varieties of manifestation are the internal world of phenomena on the other?" The sage's answer is: The very idea of two ultimate realities is self-contradictory and absurd; quite to the contrary, there can only be non-dual ultimate reality. This means that *Brahman* and *ātman* are non-different, that is, *Brahman* and *ātman* are two different *labels* for one and the same reality. But, one might ask, on what grounds is one to accept or reject the *ṛṣi*'s teaching that *Brahman* and *ātman* are non-different, one and the same reality? Before proceeding further, let us emphasize that the teaching that *Brahman* and *ātman* are non-different is the very *heart* of the Upaniṣadic wisdom. Does the *ṛṣi* anywhere show (demonstrate) the non-difference of *Brahman* and *ātman?* Or are we to just accept the teaching without inquiry and analysis? The *ṛṣi* exhorts us never to accept anyone's teaching without thoroughgoing inquiry and analysis; for to simply accept a teaching because it is proclaimed by someone who is held in high regard and veneration or because it is from a scripture and sacred writings, is to settle for second-hand truth, no matter how exalted and lofty its source. Only truth one has certified through one's own, direct, existential, and authentic experience is worthy of the title "first-hand truth." The Upaniṣadic sage exhorts us to settle for nothing less. We can read books and listen to people discourse on profound matters, but we should never accept their teachings without systematic and thorough intellectual scrutiny and direct, existential certification. An alleged truth, not so certified (or certifiable) by oneself is simply not acceptable and unworthy of the appellation "truth." For this reason, when one reads the Upaniṣads, one discovers that, after expounding on *Brahman* and *ātman,* the sage unfailingly exhorts the seeker of knowledge and wisdom, "Now that you have heard of *Brahman* (*ātman*), you should inquire into It." The Upaniṣadic sages are mystics, *par excellence,* in that they insist that nothing but direct and authentic certification can serve as the criterion for the acceptability or otherwise of anything claimed as the truth. What immediately follows is my rendition and clarification of the Upaniṣadic sage's demonstration of his teaching that *Brahman* and *ātman* are non-different; and, as the *ṛṣi* would himself have wanted and approved, I invite you to examine, analyze, and scrutinize the *ṛṣi*'s account.

The answer to the question as to how *Brahman* and *ātman* are non-different is to be found, explicitly discussed, in the famous *Māṇḍūkya Upaniṣad,* the shortest and briefest of the Upaniṣads, consisting of just twelve passages. It contains the cream, the gist, and the essence of the Upaniṣadic teaching of thoroughgoing and uncompromising non-dualism. In this Upaniṣad, the sage systematically examines the various modes of our being, namely, waking, dreaming, and deep sleep. Let it be noted that, to the best of my knowledge and belief, no Western philosophers or psychologists had ever examined the state of deep sleep; they simply dismissed it as unimportant and insignificant. To be sure, some Western psychologists, for example, Freud and Jung, did concern themselves with the study of dreams, and their inquiries into dreams were motivated by therapeutic considerations. That is, they used interpretations of dreams in order to cure various forms of mental ailments. But they never examined the *state* of dreaming itself. In sharp contrast, the Upaniṣadic inquiry into the states of waking, dreaming, and deep sleep was driven by ontological considerations — that is, by the desire to discover reality. In the waking state, one is aware of external phenomena; that is, one has external perceptions. In the dream-state, one is aware of internal phenomena; that is, one has internal perceptions. In the state of deep sleep, one is aware of neither external nor internal phenomena, that is, one has neither external nor internal perceptions. The point to be made, then, is that phenomena (objects), whether external or internal, are perceived only when the mind is functioning. In other words, perception of objects is due to the working of the mind. This means that in the state of deep sleep, where there is no perception of objects, external or internal, mind is not functioning. In a word, mind is quiescent. During the state of deep sleep, one does not know that one is in deep sleep. However, when one awakes and is asked whether one has slept well, one answers affirmatively by saying, "Yes, I have had a restful and blissful sleep." The question now is: How does one know on waking up that one has had deep sleep, if one does not know that one is in deep sleep during the state of deep sleep? It simply does not make sense to answer by saying that one *remembers* that one has had a deep sleep; for remembering implies knowing at an earlier time, but one does not know during deep sleep that one is in deep sleep. Let it be emphasized that a person's claim to have had deep sleep can be objectively confirmed or disconfirmed through neurophysiological investigation, just as his claim to have had a dream. If all knowing is through the activity of the mind — through mental operations, including remembering — and the mind is quiescent during deep sleep, then one's claim to have had deep sleep becomes mysterious and inexplicable.

The only way to rationally answer this question is to grant that there is a knowing that does not involve any mental activity — mental operations — and the knower is *consciousness* itself; and there are many passages in the Upaniṣads where "consciousness" is used synonymously with "knower" and "knowledge." Let us here clarify the two senses in which consciousness is to be understood as knowledge: 1. consciousness is the ultimate necessary condition for any knowing; that is, there cannot in principle be any knowing without consciousness, and 2. consciousness itself is knowledge. All knowing through the mind involves an *object*, the known. Accordingly, knowing through mind necessarily involves the tripartite distinction of the knower, the known, and the activity of knowing; that is, this distinction is never absent in any knowing through the mind. The upshot of these observations is that the *Māṇḍūkya Upaniṣad* recognizes and calls our attention to a knowing which does not involve the mind — mental operations. Here, the tripartite distinction mentioned above is wholly absent. In other words, in this kind of knowing, consciousness itself is the knower, and whatever is known and the activity of knowing cannot exist separately from consciousness. Thus, according to the Upaniṣadic sage, one knows, through consciousness itself, on awaking that one has had a deep sleep. It is true that on waking up mental activity resumes, and once one knows, no matter how, mind will simply report. I am fully aware that many people, in particular the Western philosophers, will dismiss as absurd the whole idea of knowing anything at all without mental operations. But let us give a clear example of knowing without involving any mental operations. Thus ask someone, say John, "Are you conscious now?" John immediately replies by saying, "Yes, of course, I am conscious. What do you mean by asking such an absurd question?" Let me clarify the situation here. Yes, there certainly are mental operations enabling John to hear the question, just as there certainly are to enable him to answer the question. But this is not the sage's point; rather, his point is, what mental operations are involved in John's *arriving* at the answer. I submit that there are none. But if someone thinks that there are mental operations, by performing which John arrived at his answer, the sage would like to see the list. It is to be emphasized that this is not a matter to be decided by arbitrary decisions and fiat of definitions, but only by experimental investigation. Let the reader inquire into this matter and determine for herself how she would arrive at her answer if she were asked this question; and if she does perform some mental operations in arriving at the answer, "I am conscious," she should give us a list of them. The Upaniṣadic sage assures her that there are absolutely no mental operations. The reason for there being no mental operations in arriving at the answer to the above question is that here *knowing and being* are one and the same and the tripartite distinction is wholly absent. One *immediately* knows that one is conscious, not through some mental operations such as inference.

The sage's point can now be stated as follows: During deep sleep, the mind is quiescent, that is, there are no mental operations and hence there can be no knowing through the mind. Nevertheless, there is consciousness and it is through consciousness itself that the deep-sleep state is known; and on waking, mental activity resumes and the mind simply reports what is known, no matter how it is known.

One might now object by saying that one's claim to have had deep sleep is based on inference — mental operations. The objection runs as follows: On waking up, one feels relaxed and attributes the state of relaxation to having had a deep sleep. This objection, however, cannot stand scrutiny. A state of relaxation can be had through means other than deep sleep. The person was awake before deep sleep and is awake after deep sleep, and when he says he has had a deep sleep he means that he was not aware of any objects in between. This claim he could not have made if he did not in some sense know that he has had a deep sleep. He could just as well have said that someone had injected into him a substance which induces relaxation.

Someone might now object by saying that the person just got up from sleep and no wonder he says that he has had a deep sleep. But this objection begs the question, for the person did not say that he has had sleep but *deep* sleep. There is no difficulty with a person's saying he has had sleep, but it is quite a different matter when he says he has had a *deep* sleep. How did he know he has had a *deep* sleep? Appeals to feeling relaxed are of no avail here, for as pointed out above a state of relaxation can be had through means other than deep sleep. The inescapable conclusion, according to the sage, is that in some sense there is knowledge of being aware of no objects at all. It might be mentioned in passing that the EEG's (electroencephalograms) of different persons in the waking state are similar, dream-states are similar, and deep-sleep states are also similar. The import of this remark is that we do not have to take on faith a person's report that he has had a deep sleep; rather, such reports are open to objective (scientific) confirmation or disconfirmation.

Another important observation here is that when we ask someone whether he slept well, he does not begin his reply by saying, "Now, well, let me see. . . ." Rather, he *immediately* says that he had trouble falling asleep, had to turn and toss in the bed for long, had bad dreams and even nightmares, or had a deep, sound, restful, and blissful sleep. This observation confirms the claim that one knows without any inference — without any mental operations — that one has had a deep sleep.

If the state of deep sleep were one wholly devoid of consciousness, then there could be no *continuity* between falling asleep and waking up, and consequently the person could not draw any inferences. This is to say that even the possibility for drawing inferences presupposes continuity of being, and, according to the *ṛṣi*, it is consciousness itself that provides the continuity. Given that the mind is quiescent during deep sleep, it is through consciousness itself (which persists even in deep sleep) that one knows directly, immediately (without having to draw any inferences) that one has had deep sleep. In short, the knower here is none other than consciousness, *ātman* itself.

The important question that now arises is: What happens to the mind during the deep-sleep state? The Upaniṣadic sage's answer is as follows: To say that the mind is quiescent during the deep-sleep state is not to say that the mind simply vanished away and became non-existent (*asat*); rather, it is to say that the mind is no longer manifest as an individual entity — a phenomenon — but became one with consciousness. It is precisely for this reason that there are no perceptions — objects — during deep sleep. In other words, during deep sleep mind merges with consciousness, losing everything characteristic of it as an individual entity. However, on waking up, mind re-emerges from consciousness, manifesting itself as an individual entity with all its specific characteristics such as thoughts, feelings, memories, etc. The point here, then, is that the knowledge that one has had deep sleep is present in consciousness and is recovered by the mind as soon as one wakes up. If the knowledge were not present, the mind could not recover it; but it is not through memory that the mind recovers the knowledge, as has been explained earlier. It is clear from these observations that the mind is none other than consciousness *with* objects. Whatever is known through the mind is always an object. In the state of deep sleep, there is no mental activity and consequently there are no objects; there is just consciousness without objects — pure, objectless consciousness. This objectless consciousness is indeed the *ātman,* which is also the knower. All objectless knowing, such as one's knowing that one is conscious and that one has had a deep sleep, is knowing by objectless consciousness, the *ātman,* not knowing by mind which is consciousness with objects.

From all the above considerations, it is clear that the Upaniṣadic sage experientially distinguishes between mind and consciousness. Whatever can be known through the mind is always, unexceptionably, an object; and whatever can be known through objectless consciousness is not an object. However, mind is not ontologically — in its being and reality — different from consciousness. In fact, it *cannot* be different from consciousness; for consciousness, *ātman,* is the ultimate non-dual reality. That is, nothing other than the non-dual reality can exist. Whatever exists is a manifestation (appearance) of consciousness, and mind is but one of the manifestations of the ultimate non-dual reality. Manifestations can disappear and reappear but consciousness — ultimate reality — whose manifestations are all appearances, itself never disappears. It is this consciousness that persists through all the three modes of our being, namely, waking, dreaming, and deep sleep. It is the source and foundation of all knowing, including knowing by mind, for there can be no knowing without consciousness. The main point emerging from the Upaniṣadic examination and analysis of the states of waking, dreaming, and deep sleep is the following: When one gets rid of everything that can be gotten rid of — in short, all perceptions, external as well as internal, as in deep sleep — there remains an ultimate residuum, the *ātman,* objectless consciousness.

At this point, let me make some pertinent observations on the treatment of the topic of consciousness in the Western tradition. In this tradition, the terms, "mind," "self," "consciousness," and "I" are used synonymously. Thus consider René Descartes (CE 1596–1650), the great French philosopher and mathematician, generally regarded as the father of Modern Western philosophy. He asks, "What then is it that I am?" and answers by saying, "A thinking thing . . . and if I entirely cease to think, thereupon I shall altogether cease to exist" ("Meditation II", *Descartes: Philosophical Writings,* tr. Norman Kemp Smith, New York: Modern Library, 1958). It is clear from this quote that Descartes does not experientially distinguish mind and consciousness. I can easily imagine an Upaniṣadic *ṛṣi* asking Descartes, "Your teaching is interesting; however, I wish to ask you as to how you *know* you cease to *exist* if you cease to *think.*" The *ṛṣi* will then offer deep sleep as an example of a state in which one certainly exists, although there is no thinking. This is the basis on which the *Māṇḍūkya Upaniṣad* experientially distinguishes mind and consciousness. We have already discussed the state of deep sleep and noted that it is the state in which there is just consciousness and absolutely no thinking; whereas in waking and dream there is consciousness with thinking, which is none other than mind. These correspond to objectless knowing and knowing objects, respectively. Failing to experientially distinguish mind and consciousness has led the Western tradition into denying objectless consciousness. In keen contrast, the Upaniṣadic sage, having experientially distinguished mind and consciousness, consistently and correctly affirms objectless consciousness — *ātman*. It is not surprising, then, that the Upaniṣadic tradition also developed various techniques — Yogic disciplines — in order to realize objectless consciousness as the ultimate non-dual reality.

Descartes never explains as to what he means by saying, "If I entirely cease to think, thereupon I shall altogether cease to exist." What precisely does he mean by "ceasing to exist?" Does he mean that he simply vanishes away and becomes non-existent? The Upaniṣadic *ṛṣi* is in a position to clarify this matter by saying, "Yes, Descartes is right in saying that upon ceasing to think he will cease to exist as *jīva, empirical ego;* but he is clearly mistaken if he means that he vanishes away and becomes non-existent. Quite to the contrary, he continues to exist as objectless consciousness." This clarification is not available to Descartes, since he failed to experientially distinguish mind and consciousness, and no wonder he is left with the absurd idea that one ceases to exist upon one's ceasing to think.

The *Māṇḍūkya Upaniṣad* goes on to discuss *turīya,* beyond the states of waking, dreaming, and deep sleep. It is worth noting that the *Māṇḍūkya Upaniṣad* does not refer to *turīya* as a state, but merely as the fourth (literal meaning of *turīya*). The reason for this is that "state" connotes duality, in particular the distinction between the knower and the known. *Turīya* is the highest mode of being, beyond all dualities. *Turīya* is just like deep sleep, except for one most important difference: whereas during deep sleep one does not know one is in deep sleep, in *turīya* one *does* know that one is in deep sleep. I shall now proceed to discuss the most significant implications of *turīya.*

In *turīya,* just as in deep sleep, there are no perceptions — objects, but one *knows* that one is in deep sleep. That is, one is aware that there are no perceptions and hence objects at all. This means that one is aware of one's being even when there are no objects at all. This is the mode of highest wakefulness. Why is it the mode of highest wakefulness? Because, the "I am" persists even when there are no objects. This in turn means that there is a reality about each of us, the same reality, non-dual consciousness — whose being is not contingent upon any objects, actual as well as potential. Such reality is indeed the necessary being, the self-existent — the reality that exists without depending for its existence upon anything other than itself. A note of caution here: In the phrase "I am" above, "I" is not to be understood as the empirical ego (*jīva*), which is an object, a phenomenon. Rather, "I" is to be correctly understood as *objectless* consciousness, pure consciousness; in a word, *ātman,* the ultimate non-dual reality. Even if the entire world of phenomena disappears, there persists a reality that never disappears and reappears, for, being unborn, uncreated, and undying, *ātman* is eternal (timeless) and immortal (that is, *ātman* always was, is, and will be).

But, one might ask, what happens to the world during deep sleep? The world does not vanish away and become non-existent; it continues to be. The reason for this is that the world is *Brahman, sat* (existence); the world is none other than the variety and multiplicity of manifestations of *Brahman.* It has no existence apart from *Brahman,* for nothing other than *Brahman* can exist and whatever exists is *Brahman.* Thus those who are awake perceive the so-called external world, and others who are asleep and dreaming perceive the so-called internal world; and for the person in deep sleep, the entire world — all manifestations — simply disappears. However, "disappear" does not mean that the world vanishes away and becomes non-existent; rather, it only means that it has become one with the unmanifest *Brahman.* If it vanishes away and becomes nothing — non-existent — it cannot appear again, as it certainly does as soon as one wakes up, with the resumption of mental activity. What all this means is that the truth proclaimed by the *ṛṣi* has to be certified by each person on her or his own. Deep sleep is thus the gift and opportunity provided by Nature, the Great Mother, for us to discover our true being as the eternal and immortal *Brahman.* Where could the world have gone? Answer: It could only have become unmanifest by merging into whatever is left as the ulti;mate residuum, namely, *ātman;* thus *Brahman,* whose manifestations are the world, is indeed *ātman,* the ultimate residuum, pure, objectless consciousness. This is indeed the demonstration that *Brahman* and *ātman* are non-different, the same non-dual reality. Since there cannot be two ultimate realities, *ātman* is *Brahman.* It should be emphasized that by its very nature the truth proclaimed by the *ṛṣi* — *ātman* and *Brahman* are non-different — has to be certified by each person; it cannot be certified for you by someone else, since another person cannot have deep sleep and *turīya* for you anymore than he or she can take a bath for you.

One might wonder as to why the *ṛṣi* uses the term "non-different" instead of "identical." The reason for this is that statement of identity implies duality, whereas statement of non-difference does not imply duality. Thus when someone says that X and Y are identical, he is implying that there are two entities X and Y which happen to be identical; in sharp contrast, when someone says Washington, D.C. and the capital of the U.S.A. are non-different, he is not referring to two different entities but rather to the same entity. *Brahman* and *ātman* are not two numerically distinguishable realities; rather, they are non-different, one and the same reality.

Turīya is the realization of ultimate non-dual reality, which is at once *ātman* (objectless consciousness) and *Brahman* (*sat*, existence); realization of this reality is the highest philosophical and religious goal the Upaniṣadic sages exhort us to attain. He who attains this realization is the most wakeful one and the realization is the *discovery* that one is immortal. Immortality is not something we need to acquire; the attainment of *turīya* is the discovery that we have always been immortal. In short, it is an epistemological discovery, that is, discovery pertaining to knowledge, not acquiring something we did not have before. Let us clarify this point by an example. Consider a person living in sheer poverty and misery. One day, while digging in his small yard, he comes upon a buried treasure. This treasure always belonged to him, but since he did not know that there is treasure buried in his yard, he has been living a life of poverty and misery. No longer is his life poor and miserable. Just so, it is because of one's ignorance that in one's true being one has always been the immortal *ātman* (*Brahman*), that one lives a miserable and impoverished life, devoid of wisdom, freedom, peace, and joy, in constant fear of death. The attainment of *turīya* sets one free of all fears and miseries, thereby enabling one to live a life of wisdom, freedom, peace, and joy.

We conclude this chapter by noting that profound neuro-physiological changes take place during the *turīya;* the electro-encephalogram shows, that during the *turīya* there is a profusion of delta waves (characteristic of deep sleep), accompanied by alpha waves, showing that the person is fully awake and extraordinarily alert.

3

Philosophical Significance

In this chapter, we shall systematically unravel and discuss the significance of the implications of non-duality to one's attempts to answer the most fundamental philosophical questions — questions concerning one's true being, the world, and ultimate reality. Towards this end, we shall begin with definitions of the central concepts of the Upaniṣadic teaching.

Reality (*sat*). That which exists without depending for its existence upon anything other than itself. That is, reality is self-existent, and reality is none other than *Brahman*. Since nothing other than *Brahman* can in principle exist, *Brahman* exists without depending for its existence upon anything other than itself.

Phenomena (appearances). All phenomena are appearances of *Brahman;* it is worth reminding the reader here that a phenomenon is anything that is or can in principle be an object of consciousness. All phenomena exist in time, although some phenomena also exist in space. Thus all the so-called external phenomena, such as tables, chairs, people, stars, galaxies, etc. exist in both space and time; whereas the so-called internal phenomena, such as thoughts, emotions, mental images, including dreams, exist in time only. The point here, then, is that all phenomena, whether external or internal, have in common the fact of *existence.* This existence is *Brahman, sat.* Thus phenomena have no existence apart from *Brahman;* they are indeed the appearances of *Brahman,* reality. Phenomena, being time-bound, arise and pass away; whereas *Brahman,* being timeless, never arises and passes away. On the contrary, *Brahman* always was, is, and will be.

Unreality (*asat*). Unreality can never, in principle, be an object of our consciousness; thus X is unreal just in case the concept of X is self-contradictory. Examples of unreality are: married bachelor, son of a barren woman, square-circle, and so on. Unreality never existed, nor does it exist now, nor can it exist in the future. This is precisely what is meant by the Upaniṣadic declaration that *asat* can never become *sat*, just as *sat* can never become *asat*.

One might now ask, "What is the status of phenomena; are they real or unreal?" In order to answer this question, we need to introduce and discuss a profound notion, called "sublation," formulated by the great Śaṅkara, the founder of the school of Advaita Vedānta (non-dualistic Vedānta).

Sublation is essentially the mental process of correcting and rectifying errors of judgement. Thus one is said to sublate a previously-held judgement when, in the light of a new experience which contradicts it, one regards the judgement as false or disvalues it in some significant sense. It is obvious that sublation of a given judgement necessarily results in its being replaced by a new one. Not only judgements but also concepts, relations, and in general any object of consciousness can be sublated. For Śaṅkara, sublatability is the criterion of the ontological status — the reality — of any object of consciousness; anything that is in principle sublatable is of a lesser degree of reality and value than that which replaces it as a result of sublation. It is through this concept of sublation that Śaṅkara arrives at his ontological hierarchy of reality, phenomena (appearances), and unreality.

Sublation presupposes an essential dualism between the experiencer and the experienced, the subject and the object; sublation also presupposes a plurality of objects, concepts, judgements — contents of consciousness in general. The distinction of subject and object is necessary for sublation because it is the subject which sublates the object, whether a concept or a judgement. Plurality of objects is necessary for sublation, because sublation analytically implies juxtaposing one object or experience against another incompatible object or experience and judging that the first has a lesser degree of reality or value than the second. In the light of these observations, to say that the experience of reality (*Brahman*) is unsublatable, is to say that no other experience can conceivably contradict the experience of reality. The reason for this is that nothing other than reality exists; further, reality is devoid of all distinctions — not only the distinction between one object and another but also that between the subject and object, the self and the non-self. Thus the experience of reality (*Brahman*) transcends all distinctions and is therefore the experience of pure non-duality between the subject and the object, the self and the non-self. It is clear that the experience of reality is unsublatable, since there can be nothing besides the non-dual experience which may conceivably controvert the experience. Reality, *Brahman,* is unsublatable because it is wholly bereft of any distinctions, oppositions, qualifications, or relations. It is the experience of reality that sublates all else, itself being unsublatable by any other experience whatsoever. In terms of value, there can in principle be no experience more valuable than the experience of reality, *Brahman.*

Appearance (phenomenon) is that which in principle can be sublated. In contrast with reality as Existence (*sat*), appearance may be construed as the realm of existents, *entities* that exist, actually and potentially. Existents can be classified into three kinds: 1. real existents, 2. existents, and 3. illusory existents. Real existents are those which can only be sublated by reality. Unlike reality, real existents are experienced in the matrix of subject-object distinction. It follows, then, that the only experience which can sublate the experience of a real existent is that which transcends the subject-object dichotomy — in short, the experience of reality. Let us illustrate this point by two examples. In the religious context, the human being experiences himself or herself as a creature and God as the Creator, towards whom he or she has an attitude of dependency, devotion, and obedience. This experience of the dualism between creator and creature cannot be sublated by any experience within the realm of variety and plurality. It is only the experience of reality as transcending names and forms, and hence all distinctions, that can sublate the experience of the distinction between creator and creature (*Vedānta-Sūtras of Bādarāyaṇa, with the Commentary by Śaṅkara,* hereafter cited as *VS,* II. 1.22, tr. George Thibaut, New York: Dover Publications, 1970). To take another example, one accepts the law of non-contradiction as the touchstone of prepositional truth (truth of a sentence or claim); that is, one takes a sentence p as true insofar as not-p is false and vice versa. And as long as we organize and analyze our experience of the world in accordance with the law of non-contradiction, no proposition, and hence no truth we formulate, can conceivably violate or sublate the principle of non-contradiction. Only the experience of reality wholly transcending logic and language can sublate the principle of non-contradiction. This observation has far-reaching consequences to the enterprise of rational-scientific knowledge. The mind can grasp neither itself nor reality. It can only function by drawing distinctions, and for it to grasp itself, it should function without drawing any distinctions — a self-contradiction. In a word, mind cannot catch itself, just as a knife which cuts everything else cannot cut itself and the eye which sees everything else cannot see itself. The mind cannot grasp reality, because reality wholly transcends the realm of the mind — the realm of distinctions. The second category under appearances is existent. Whereas a real existent can only be sublated by reality, an existent can be sublated by a real existent as well as by reality. The domain of existents can simply be characterized as that of conventional knowledge, knowledge based on rules and canons agreed upon by conventions, which may be commonsensical, logical, scientific, social, etc. Thus, for example, from the point of view of common sense I assert that my desk is a solid body. But this commonsensical view is sublated by the scientific claim that the desk is a colony of electrical charges in constant motion with empty space between them. That is, the commonsensical notion of solid body is replaced by the scientific notion of moving electrical charges. And the notion of moving electrical charges is sublated by the experience of reality as being above and beyond all distinctions. This is what is meant by saying that an existent may be sublated by another existent or by reality. But since all real existents are sublatable by reality, it follows that sublation is a transitive relation with respect to existents, real existents, and reality. Thus let X be an existent, Y a real existent, and Z reality; then "Z sublates Y and Y sublates X" implies "Z sublates X."

The third category of appearances (phenomena) is illusory existent, which can be sublated by all other kinds of experience. Under illusory existents come illusions, hallucinations, dreams, and all erroneous perceptions. An illusory existent is distinguished by the fact that it fails to fulfil the criteria for empirical, everyday, conventional truth. Thus, a thirsty man travelling in a desert rushes to a certain spot to quench his thirst. But on reaching the spot, he finds that there is no water and realizes that his perception of water is an illusory perception, a mirage, which fails to meet the criteria for water as existent. Consequently, the *advaitin* (non-dualist) says that the experience of the mirage is sublated by another experience.

We come now to the concept of unreality. Unreality neither can nor cannot be sublated by other experiences. Anything which cannot in principle be an object of our experience, actual or possible, is unreal. For anything to be sublatable, it must in principle be an object of our experience, actual or potential; and since the unreal, such as a married bachelor and the son of a barren woman, can never in principle be an object of our experience, it would be misleading to say that the unreal is sublatable or not sublatable. For this reason, Śaṅkara teaches that unreal objects are neither sublatable nor non-sublatable. It is worth noting here that an illusory existent, for example a mirage, is one which *as a matter of fact* does not have an objective counterpart in our experience, whereas an unreal object is one which *in principle cannot* have an objective counterpart. In short, the unreal is non-existent, non-being (*asat*).

We are now ready to answer the question, "What is the status of phenomena, are they real or unreal?" Phenomena are neither real nor unreal. They are not real, because, unlike reality, they are sublatable; they are not unreal, either, because, unlike unreality, phenomena *are* objects of our experience, actual as well as possible. Phenomena thus have an intermediate status. Let us illustrate all of this through an analogy. Consider once again jars and dishes made of clay; the jars and dishes are appearances of clay. Imagine someone first making a jar and then breaking the jar and making a dish; what has happened? The judgement "this is a jar" is sublated by the judgement "this is a dish." Now imagine the person destroying the dish he just made by destroying the jar; although the jar and the dish have disappeared, the clay of which they were made has not disappeared. That is, the jar and the dish are both sublated by the clay. Jars and dishes may appear, disappear, and reappear, but the clay always remains the same; phenomena are like the jars, dishes, and so on, and reality is like the clay. The clay itself does not undergo any real change, that is, it does not cease to be clay; only forms and names change — what was previously called "a jar" is now called "a dish." Further, the jars and dishes have no existence (being) apart from the clay, they are dependent on the clay. That is, the existence of jars and dishes is dependent upon the existence of the clay; in keen contrast, the existence of the clay is in no way dependent on jars and dishes. In a similar manner, all phenomena exist by depending for their existence upon *Brahman* (*sat,* existence), whereas *Brahman* Itself is not dependent upon the existence of phenomena. All phenomena are thus the variety and multiplicity of the appearances of *Brahman,* the self-existent. It needs to be emphasized that even illusions are grounded in reality; that is, illusory experiences — perceptions — cannot be had arbitrarily and capriciously, but only when certain objective conditions are fulfilled — one cannot expect to experience a mirage in one's closet. Do jars and dishes exist? Yes, they certainly do; they are objects of our consciousness, and therefore are not unreal, like a square-circle or the son of a barren woman. But do they exist independently? Are they self-existents? They cannot exist independently of the clay, and therefore are not self-existents. They have absolutely no existence — no being — apart from the existence of the clay. Thus all phenomena are *Brahman* (reality, the self-existent), in that they are all merely the appearances — manifestations — of *Brahman*. Phenomena appear, disappear, and reappear, but *Brahman* Itself never disappears. *Brahman* always was, is, and will be. Just as the clay does not undergo any real change in appearing as jars, dishes, and so on, so also *Brahman* does not undergo any real change in appearing as phenomena. *Brahman* does not undergo any real change in appearing as variety of phenomena, because nothing other than *Brahman* can exist and whatever exists is *Brahman,* and hence *Brahman* can never become something other than Itself. *Brahman,* being timeless, does not undergo any real change, unlike phenomena — appearances — which, being time-bound, do undergo changes, changes in forms and names. *Brahman,* transcending the senses and intellect, is timeless, formless, and nameless.

Thus, according to the Upaniṣadic teaching, *Brahman* is both the material and efficient cause of the world of phenomena. *Brahman* is the material cause of all phenomena, because phenomena have no being (existence) apart from *Brahman;* and *Brahman* is the efficient cause of phenomena, because there is nothing other than *Brahman* which *makes Brahman* appear as phenomena. This teaching that the effect — the world of phenomena — pre-exists in or non-different from the cause, namely *Brahman,* is known as *satkāryavāda. Brahman* and the world of phenomena are *non-different;* they are not two numerically distinguishable realities. Rather, the world of phenomena — of our senses and mind — is simply the actual and possible appearances, manifestations, of *Brahman,* the non-dual reality, besides which nothing can in principle exist. If *Brahman* is the cause of the world and if the world as the effect is different from, or other than, its cause (*Brahman*), then it is clear that there exists in the effect something that was not in the cause.

This means that there is something other than *Brahman,* in direct violation of the central Upaniṣadic insight that nothing other than *Brahman* can in principle exist, because *Brahman* is Existence, actual as well as potential. Hence the conclusion that there cannot, in principle, be anything in the effect that was not in the cause (*satkāryavāda*).

The Upaniṣadic claim that all change is change only in name and form is known in Śaṅkara's Advaita Vedānta (non-dualistic Vedānta) as *vivartavāda* (doctrine of apparent changes). This claim rests on the fundamental insight that forms do not and cannot have any reality of their own; their reality is inseparable from and dependent upon Existence (*Brahman*), just as the forms known as "jar" and "dish" cannot have any existence of their own, apart from the existence of the clay. According to Śaṅkara, we cannot even conceive of what it is for a form to exist apart from that of which it is a form. As such, to regard changes in form as real is to think that that of which it is a form itself undergoes real changes. Śaṅkara therefore concludes that all changes in form and name are only apparent changes (*vivartavāda*). In brief, changes in form and name are not changes in reality but only in appearance. It may be noted that this argument for the apparent nature of changes can easily be extended to qualities. Qualities are inseparable from that of which they are qualities. If a thing and its quality are two distinct and independent realities, we need a third reality to relate the thing and the quality. But then we need a fourth reality to relate the third to the first two, and so on *ad infinitum.* According to Śaṅkara, the only way out of this threat of infinite regress is to regard qualities, not as independent reality, but as inseparable from and dependent upon that of which they are qualities. Only changes in reality, of which something is a quality, can be said to be real changes. But since reality, *Brahman,* cannot undergo any real changes and become something other than *Brahman,* it follows that all changes in qualities are merely *apparent* changes.

We shall now discuss how the criterion of sublation and *vivartavāda,* conjoined with the concepts of *māyā, avidyā,* and *adhyāsa,* lead to the central Upaniṣadic teaching that *Brahman* is the sole reality and the world of our senses and intellect, the world of phenomena, is merely an appearance.

Māyā. The term *māyā* is often translated as "illusion." However, such a translation is extremely misleading and is the source of serious misunderstandings of Advaita Vedānta (non-dualistic Vedānta). The concept of *māyā* is best clarified by setting forth its psychological, epistemological, and ontological meanings. Needless to point out, there are analytical connections among the three kinds of meaning. Psychologically speaking, *māyā* is our persistent tendency to regard appearances as reality and vice versa. In terms of the criterion of sublatability, *māyā* is our constant propensity to regard the sublatable as the unsublatable and vice versa. From an epistemological point of view — point of view pertaining to knowledge — *māyā* is our ignorance (*avidyā*) as to the difference between appearance and reality. Reality is that which cannot in principle be sublated by any other experience, whereas appearance is that which in principle can be sublated by other experiences. Sublation is possible, as we have pointed out earlier, only where distinctions exist; and since reality transcends all distinctions, the experience of reality cannot in principle be sublated. On the other hand, the realm of appearances is necessarily one of distinctions and is therefore sublatable. Consequently, one appearance can be sublated by another, and all appearances can be sublated by reality. It is only by being unaware of this distinction between the sublatable and the unsublatable that human beings mistakenly believe that appearances are reality. In other words, ignorance as to the nature of reality is the foundation of *māyā.* It is clear from all these observations that only the unsublatable, undifferentiated *sat* (existence) is reality. The changing world of our senses, emotions, and intellect is merely an appearance. *Māyā* is beginningless and endless, unthinkable and inexpressible. *Māyā* is unthinkable because all thinking has its origin in it, and inexpressible because language has its basis in it. *Māyā* is thus the warp and woof of the world of appearances — the world of senses, intellect, and emotion.

From an ontological point of view — that is, in terms of reality — *māyā* is the creative power of reality (*Brahman*) by virtue of which the world of variety and multiplicity comes into existence. Sometimes *māyā* as the creative power of reality is referred to as "the sheer playfulness (*līlā*) of reality."

Thus when the Upaniṣadic sage refers to the phenomenal world as *māyā* in the sense of illusion, he is not saying that the phenomenal world is unreal, but that it is an appearance, which has its foundation in reality. Appearance, unlike unreality, is sublatable. For this reason, there can be no such thing as pure illusion. Every illusion is grounded in reality. In other words, illusions and appearances, unlike unreality, are not pure nothing, non-being, non-existence. The very fact that illusions are sublatable shows that they are genuine components of our experience. It is clear, then, that when the *advaitin* (non-dualist) says that the phenomenal world is an illusion, he is not saying that it is non-existent and unreal; quite to the contrary, he is affirming that the phenomenal world, like illusions, is not an independent, self-existing reality but is grounded through and through in the sole reality of *Brahman*.

Avidyā. The term *avidyā* means ignorance, which may be characterized as not only not knowing the real but also thinking that appearances are real. Sometimes Śaṅkara and other *advaitins* speak of *māyā* and ignorance interchangeably. This is quite understandable in view of the fact that *māyā* in one of its senses means our persistent tendency to regard appearances as real and vice versa. Like *māyā*, ignorance is beginningless and endless. From a logical point of view, *māyā* and ignorance are coeval, in that there cannot be the one without the other. However, from an epistemological point of view, ignorance may be regarded as prior to *māyā*, in that the latter presupposes the former. That is, ignorance is the necessary condition for *māyā*. This also means that *māyā* vanishes away as soon as ignorance is overcome by knowledge of the real. The magician's trick best illustrates this point. A magician makes one thing appear as another or apparently produces something out of nothing. The point here is that it is we, the spectators, being ignorant of the magician's trick, who mistake appearances for reality. For the magician himself, as the master of the trick, there can be no illusion, no sense of surprise and amazement. But once we discover the trick by which the magician makes things appear, disappear, and reappear, we no longer fall victim to illusion but recognize the magician's performance for what it is. Just as the magician, by his power of manipulation, creates in us illusions, so also reality (*Brahman*) by its creative power, namely *māyā*, produces in us the illusion of the phenomenal world of variety, multiplicity, and diversity. Once ignorance is overcome by knowledge of the real, one is no longer held captive by *māyā*. One might now ask, "How is ignorance produced?" In order to answer this question, we turn to Śaṅkara's concept of *adhyāsa*.

Adhyāsa (superimposition). The literal meaning of *adhyāsa* is "superimposition," which Śaṅkara defines as "the apparent presentation, in the form of remembrance, to consciousness of something previously observed in something else" (*VS* I.1). As an act, superimposition is our thinking mistakenly that an object has certain characteristics which in fact it does not have. In general, we may say that superimposition consists in attributing qualities not immediately presented to consciousness to a thing that is immediately given to consciousness. The classic illustration of superimposition is the rope-snake example. A man steps on a rope in the dark and thinks it is a snake. Here the rope is what is immediately present to consciousness, the snake is an object of past experience, and superimposition is the person's mistakenly attributing the remembered qualities of the snake to the rope. The present experience of the rope and the past experience of a snake are necessary conditions for one to be able mistakenly to claim that what is now experienced is a snake. In other words, the snake-like experience cannot be had in the absence of the rope. But when one brings a lamp and discovers that what one has stepped on is only a rope, one's snake-like experience is recognized as being illusory. In a similar manner, the empirical world — the world of phenomena — arises as a result of our superimposing qualities on the undifferentiated, formless, nameless, and unsublatable reality (*Brahman*), Just as under superimposition the rope is experienced as a snake, so also, under the superimposition of names and forms, reality, which is beyond names and forms, is experienced as the world of appearances. On attaining knowledge of reality, ignorance, *māyā*, and the world of appearances vanish away simultaneously. It is clear by now that superimposition is the source of ignorance. One can talk about *adhyāsa* in two senses: 1. with respect to particular experiences in the world of appearances, and 2. with respect to the world of appearances in general. In the former case, *adhyāsa* is the attribution of qualities remembered to a thing now being experienced. In the latter case, *adhyāsa* is the superimposition of names and forms on the nameless and formless non-dual reality. We might mention here that the *advaitin* also distinguishes between two kinds of ignorance: primordial (universal) ignorance and individual (temporary) ignorance. The former has neither beginning nor end, whereas the latter can be ended by the individual's attaining knowledge of the real. Moreover, universal ignorance serves to account for the *common* world of appearances. That all human beings agree that there is a world of phenomena is thus due to the fact that all human beings are equally afflicted with ignorance. Interestingly enough, it is this common ignorance that makes possible talk of the *objective* existence of the world and *objective* truths thereof.

Having explicated the central epistemological concepts of Advaita Vedānta, as systematized by Śaṅkara, we are now in a position to present the *advaitin*'s account of *Brahman*, *ātman*, and the phenomenal world.

According to the criterion of sublatability, *Brahman* is the sole reality — that which cannot be sublated by any other experience. That is to say, *Brahman* transcends all distinctions, such as subject and object and self and non-self. Consequently, *Brahman* is unthinkable, imperceivable, and inexpressible. *Brahman* can only be experienced in non-perceptual, non-conceptual, direct, intuitive insight — *prajñā*.

The world of phenomena is the realm of *māyā*, the product of ignorance, which in turn is generated by our superimposing names and forms on the non-dual, unsublatable, nameless, and formless reality, *Brahman*. The world of our senses and intellect is thus the world of appearances. This is not to say, however, that the world of appearances is unreal; on the contrary, since the world of appearances is sublatable by reality (*Brahman*), it is not non-being (non-existent) and unreality (*VS* II.2.28). Just as a man stepping on a rope in the dark thinks in his ignorance that it is a snake that he has stepped on, so also man, in his ignorance of the nameless and formless *Brahman*, thinks that the changing world of appearances is the reality. What, then, one might ask, is the status of the snake the man thinks he has stepped on? Is it real or unreal? Or, on a cosmic scale, what is the status of the world of appearances? Is it real or unreal? According to the *advaitin*, the snake is neither real nor unreal. It is not real, because it can be sublated; it is not unreal, because if it were it neither could nor could not be sublated. Similarly, the world of appearances is neither real nor unreal. Hence the hierarchy: the unreal, the neither real nor the unreal, and the real. Further, just as no snake-like experience is possible without the empirical reality of the rope, so also there can be no experience of the world of appearances without the underlying reality of *Brahman*. Most importantly, just as there are no two numerically distinguishable realities called "the rope" and "the snake" but only one reality, the rope appearing as snake under certain conditions of superimposition, so also there are no two numerically distinguishable realities called "the world of appearances" and *Brahman* but only the non-dual reality *Brahman,* which appears to us as the phenomenal world under the superimposition of names and forms. When we free ourselves from ignorance and therewith *māyā,* the world of appearances itself will be seen as *Brahman.*

According to the *advaitin, ātman,* the inmost Self of the human being, is pure undifferentiated consciousness. Like *Brahman, ātman* is nameless and formless and hence spaceless, timeless, imperceivable, unthinkable, and inexpressible. It is the silent witness of the world of change and appearance. Like *Brahman, ātman* transcends all distinctions. Consequently, it is reality, unsublatable by any other experience. Human beings in their ignorance mistakenly identify the *ātman* with one or other of the appearances (names and forms), such as the body, the mind, and so on. *Ātman* as reality is none of these things. Just as in the case of *Brahman, ātman* cannot be an object in the world of appearances alongside other objects; on the contrary, it is the light which illuminates all objects (that which cannot be seen by the eye but that by which the eye sees, etc.). How does one establish the existence of *ātman?* One can never deny *ātman;* it is not given to anyone to be able to proclaim, "I am not conscious." The empirical ego, *jīva,* is simply the appearance of *ātman* under limiting conditions of the body-mind (psycho-physiological) complex.

Ātman and *Brahman* are not two numerically distinguishable realities; rather they are two different labels for one and the same reality. For this reason, knowledge of *Brahman* coincides with knowledge of *ātman.* One experiences *Brahman* as the sole unsublatable reality when one transcends all distinctions, in particular that between the subject and object. The subject and object coalesce into each other; the subject is also the object and vice versa. In such an experience, *Brahman,* the timeless reality underlying the changing world of external appearances, is also *ātman,* the timeless reality underlying the world of internal appearances. In other words, where all distincrions between the external and the internal vanish away, the distinction between the Self and the non-Self also vanishes away and one experiences Pure Existence as Pure Consciousness. Such an experience is also one of Pure Bliss. For this reason, Advaita Vedānta refers to the experience of the non-dual reality (*Brahman, ātman*) as *saccidānanda* (*sat* = Pure Existence, *cit* = Pure Consciousness, *ānanda* = Pure Bliss). It should be emphasized that one should not hereby think that *saccidānanda* is a description of (*Brahman, ātman*); the reason for this is that *Brahman*, being formless, nameless, and non-dual, defies any description (only objects can be described). Thus *saccidānanda* is most properly understood as description of one's *experience* of *Brahman*, not as description of *Brahman* Itself.

Brahman and *ātman* are thus non-different, one and the same. (Remember the Upaniṣadic passage: "What is within is also what is without, and what is without is also what is within; and whosoever sees any difference between what is within and what is without goes evermore from death to death." *Kaṭha* II.iv.10.) It is because of its emphatic rejection of any difference between *ātman* and *Brahman*, Self and non-Self, that the Upaniṣadic teaching, as systematized and proclaimed by Śaṅkara, is known as Advaita Vedānta. *Advaita* means non-dualistic and is not to be translated as "monistic." The reason for this is that no positive attributes can be predicated of reality (*Brahman, ātman*); one can only say what it is not. Thus to say that reality is non-dual is not the same as saying that it is one (see our earlier discussion on number and plurality). The Upaniṣadic *ṛṣi*'s teaching should therefore be correctly referred to as Advaita Vedānta.

4

Philosophical Significance (continued)

WHAT is the nature of knowledge of phenomena? How is it different from knowledge of the ultimate non-dual reality, *Brahman* (*ātman*)? In order to clearly answer these questions, we need to discuss the principle of two kinds of knowledge and truth, the lower and the higher, originally formulated in the *Muṇḍaka Upaniṣad.* Our discussion begins with a clarification of knowledge through the concept of categorial framework, to a consideration of which I shall now turn.

All thinking begins somewhere and where it begins depends upon the background of the thinker and the sorts of things the thinker is interested in inquiring into. Thus it is only natural that some things are included in and others are excluded from one's inquiry. By the term "categorial framework," I mean the matrix in which inquiry takes place and knowledge-claims are made. A categorial framework thus underlies every system of knowledge, whether in science, philosophy, or religion. Every categorial framework consists of certain presuppositions, concepts, categories, definitions, axioms, postulates, a system of logic, and criteria for judging the truth or falsity of knowledge-claims and hence for their acceptance or rejection. Further, every categorial framework is associated with (or points to) a certain world-view. Thus, for example, one can speak of the Platonic, Aristotelian, Augustinian, Sāṁkhyan, Buddhist, Hegelian, Bergsonian, Whiteheadian categorial frameworks. It is worth noting here that it is usually philosophers who construct and articulate particular categorial frameworks. A philosopher who constructs a categorial framework also attempts to justify it. Such a justification, following Immanuel Kant (CE 1724–1804), is known as "transcendental deduction." Transcendental deduction consists of showing that 1. the particular categorial framework under consideration is the one actually employed by people to produce objective knowledge of the world, and 2. the categorial framework is the *only one* capable of enabling us to obtain objective knowledge of the world (uniqueness-demonstration).

Before proceeding further, it will be in order to distinguish three levels of knowledge. Level-1 consists of knowledge of objects (phenomena) constituting a certain domain, for example, physics, and various specialties within physics, such as astronomy, low-temperature physics, nuclear physics, and so on; or biology and the many specialties therein. Level-2 consists of knowledge of the foundations of a given discipline at Level-1, foundations in the sense that they make possible the discipline (give rise to and support the discipline) and lend to the discipline its specific form, content, and character. In the light of our earlier characterization of a categorial framework, the foundations of any discipline at Level-1 may be referred to as "categorial framework." Someone may be a physicist in the sense of one who investigates some subset(s) of phenomena constituting the domain of physics, but she may not have inquired into the foundations of her own discipline and therefore may either be wholly unaware of its foundations or only have vague and unclear notions about them. Most scientists, including some very successful ones, are of this kind. This remark is not to be construed as an insult or accusation but only as a statement of fact. However, it is often the case that only those scientists who also inquire into the foundations of their disciplines make original and radical contributions to the advancement of their fields — for example, Galileo, Newton, Darwin, Einstein, Bohr, Schrodinger, and Heisenberg, to mention only a few of the truly great scientists. Level-3 goes beyond knowledge of particular categorial frameworks underlying particular disciplines to knowledge of the nature of knowledge producible through categorial frameworks. Knowledge based on categorial frameworks may simply be called "categorial knowledge." Level-3 knowledge, then, is knowledge concerning the nature of *all* categorial knowledge — categorial knowledge in general. A categorial framework may also be referred to as "perceptual-conceptual framework." The notion of categorial framework stems from the profound insight that the kind of knowledge a certain kind of beings are capable of producing is inextricably bound up with their psycho-physiological make-up. This means, first, that among various kinds of beings human beings, constitute only one, and second, the nature and limits of human knowledge is governed by the physiological and psychological constitution of the human being. This is the same as saying that, had human beings been of a different psycho-physiological make-up than their present one, the nature and limits of knowledge they produce would be different (from that which they now, as a matter of fact, produce). There should be nothing surprising about this claim. Simply imagine our optic nerves being arranged differently; then it is only to be expected that our experience of colours would have been different from our present experience of them. Similar is the case with regard to our other sense organs. It is obvious, then, that our perceptions are ineluctably bound up with the constitution of our perceptual apparatus. To take another example, we are the kind of beings who cannot see the back of an object simultaneously with its front. That is, if I hold up an object, say a book, in front of you, you can only see its front but not its back. There is nothing mysterious about this observation; on the contrary, it is a correct report about our ways of perceiving. We also know that changes in our biochemical make-up result in changes in our perceptions. It is a fact, then, that our perceptions are a function of our physiological constitution. Our claims as to what sorts of things make up the world and what properties they possess, and what relations obtain among them is a function of our physiological make-up.

But, in addition to our physiological make-up, our psychological constitution determines the nature of the knowledge we produce. The term "psychological" here is to be understood as encompassing the mental and the emotional. In short, the psychological consists of the sentient and the sapient, the emotional and the mental, respectively. What comes to us through our sense organs is ordered and organized — categorized — according to our psychological constitution. It goes without saying that beings endowed with a different psychological constitution than we are will organize and categorize differently what they receive through their sense organs, thereby resulting in knowledge-claims different from ours. It is to be noted that our psychological make-up allows for a variety of ways of organizing and categorizing, each way being appropriate to a certain end and purpose. All the possible different ways of ordering, organizing, and categorizing that which comes through our sensory channels and equipment define the "range of our psychological make-up."

It should be clear from the above that as human beings we are capable of perceptions and conceptions, actual and potential, lying within a certain range determined by our psycho-physiological constitution. We may refer to this range as "perceptual-conceptual range."

The knowledge-claims a thinker advances are constituted of percepts and concepts allowed for (permitted by, falling within the range of) by the categorial framework with which he conducts his inquiry. This is the reason why a categorial framework may be referred to as "perceptual-conceptual framework."

In the light of the above, we are now in a position to make the following fundamental observations concerning the nature of categorial knowledge:

1. All commonsensical and rational-scientific knowledge is through and through categorial knowledge; by this I mean that every expressible and communicable knowledge-claim, whether in everyday life, science, philosophy, or religion, is necessarily

(inevitably) bound up with some categorial framework or other. This is the same as saying that no expressible and communicable knowledge-claim is in principle possible apart from and independently of some categorial framework; that is, every expressible and communicable knowledge-claim is *relative to* (*dependent upon*) a categorial framework.

2. It would therefore be a serious mistake to lay absolute claims on behalf of any categorial knowledge.

3. However, each thinker, being ignorant of this fact, makes *absolute* claims on behalf of knowledge generated by her own categorial framework and condemns the knowledge-claims of other thinkers (conducting their inquiries with different frameworks) as false.

4. In this manner arise conflict and opposition among thinkers; simply imagine the battles being constantly waged against each other by thinkers, Aristotelians against Platonists, Humeans against Kantians, idealists against realists, substance-philosophers against process-philosophers, empiricists against rationalists, theists against atheists, Western philosophers against non-Western philosophers, and so on. It is to be emphasized that, contrary to the widespread but uncritical belief, such conflicts also exist in the scientific enterprise — as witness the opposition between Ptolemaic astronomy (geocentric system) and Copernican astronomy (heliocentric system), between Aristotelian physics and the physics of Galileo and Newton, between Newtonian physics and Einsteinian physics, between classical physics and quantum physics, between Creationism and Darwinian biology, and so on. The conflict between one system (theory) and another is traceable to the conflict and incompatibility between the world-views (paradigms) underlying the systems. The term "paradigm" is generally used when one talks about conflicts between competing scientific theories. A paradigm is essentially a categorial framework, although it is worth emphasizing that, rigorously speaking, a categorial framework is much wider than a paradigm, in the sense that a categorial framework encompasses a paradigm (and not the converse).

5. Transcendental deductions of categorial frameworks are in

principle impossible, according to the Upaniṣadic sages, including Śaṅkara. Although it is quite easy, through sociological research, to show that, as a matter of fact, people use a certain framework to produce objective knowledge of the world, the second part of transcendental deduction — uniqueness-demonstration — cannot be accomplished. Uniqueness-demonstration consists of showing that a certain categorial framework is the *only* framework which enables us to produce objective knowledge of the world. The advocate of the framework cannot, in principle, establish this, and every argument to establish this is necessarily (inevitably) circular and therefore question-begging and fruitless. For, in order to demonstrate that the world is as described by his own framework, the thinker needs to know what the world is like independently of his framework, and then show that his framework does indeed describe the world faithfully. Is it not true that if I showed you a photograph and asked whether it is a picture of my friend John X, you cannot answer unless you have seen him at least once? Just so, unless one knows what the world is like independently of categorial frameworks, one cannot sensibly claim that the world is indeed as described by one's own framework. For this reason, every argument the thinker constructs for demonstrating the uniqueness-claim necessarily employs the categories of the very framework (for, on his own admission, there are none else), which in the first place needs justification. The incontrovertible conclusion, then, is that transcendental deductions are in principle impossible.

6. It should be quite clear by now that, broadly speaking, commonsensical and scientific knowledge is Level-1 knowledge. Philosophical inquiry is concerned with the construction and examination of particular categorial frameworks; and the knowledge-claims of philosophers are also categorial. However, there is a fundamental difference between the knowledge-claims of science and those of philosophy. A philosopher, unlike a scientist, is usually concerned with saying something about ultimate reality, and he does this by elevating some category of his own framework to an ultimate status. Hence such philosophical proclamations as: Ultimate reality is of the nature of substance, of

the nature of process; ultimate reality is of the essence of mind, of spirit; ultimate reality is material (constituted of elementary particles); ultimate reality is one; ultimate reality is plural; ultimate reality is a person; and so on. But the point here is that philosophical inquiry is essentially inquiry at Level-2 knowledge. We shall examine later the nature and significance of knowledge at Level-3.

7. To say that all rational-scientific truths are bound up with some framework or other is to say that they are all *relative* truths; "relative" here is to be understood as relative to some framework or other and hence to beings of a certain psycho-physiological constitution. But there are many who uncritically equate relative truth with falsehood. "Relative truth" means truth certifiable by all inquirers who are similarly constituted and conduct their inquiry according to a certain categorial framework. Thus, for example, when an American physicist advances a knowledge-claim, say, electrons are negatively charged particles, a Japanese physicist, operating with the same framework with which the American physicist operates, certifies that knowledge-claim to be true. It is to be emphasized that a knowledge-claim has neither meaning nor truth (nor falsity) apart from (independently of) a categorial framework. Thus objective truth is not truth which has nothing to do with us but rather is truth certifiable by different inquirers who are constituted alike and conduct their inquiry according to a certain framework. Put pointedly, objective truth is no more and no less than *intersubjective* truth.

8. What about universal truth? Once again, many people mistakenly equate universal truth with absolute truth. Universal truth is relative truth that has received over a period of time certification by larger and larger numbers of inquirers the world over. Universal truth is *not* absolute truth, for *absolute* truth means truth that is independent of the constitutions of the inquirers and hence independent of any and all categorial frameworks. In the light of our characterization of categorial framework, it follows that there simply cannot be any categorial truth which can be claimed to be absolute truth. If there is any absolute truth at all, one thing must be very clear:

It cannot, in principle, be captured in any categorial framework by *any* inquirer. That is, absolute truth, if there be such, transcends all categorial frameworks and all inquirers, actual and potential, here as well as elsewhere. Only those who are ignorant of the nature of categorial knowledge mistake some categorial truth for absolute truth.

I come now to a discussion of knowledge at Level-3. We have earlier stated that knowledge at Level-3 is knowledge of the nature of categorial knowledge in general — knowledge producible through any and all categorial frameworks. Thus all the points listed above are part and parcel of knowledge at Level-3. Philosophers do not usually conduct inquiry into Level-3 knowledge, for they are too absorbed in and preoccupied with defending their own frameworks and laying absolute claims on behalf of their own categorial knowledge-claims, thereby becoming embroiled in interminable philosophical disputes, disagreements, and controversies. But we have seen earlier that one of the central insights of the Upaniṣadic teaching is that we superimpose names and forms (*nāma* and *rūpa*) on a formless and nameless reality and thereby generate categorial frameworks and categorial truths. This superimpositional activity is known as *adhyāsa* in *Śaṅkara.* It is obvious that *adhyāsa* is the source of all categorial frameworks, and the super-impositional activities of differently constituted beings result in different categorial frameworks and therewith different knowledge-claims. Before proceeding further, let us state the principle of two kinds of knowledge and truth as articulated in the *Muṇḍaka Upaniṣad:*

> There are two kinds of knowledge, the higher and the lower. The lower is knowledge of the Veda (the *Ṛg,* the *Sāma,* the *Yajur,* and the *Atharva*), and also of phonetics, ceremonials, grammar, etymology, metre and astronomy. The higher knowl edge is of that by which one knows the changeless reality. By this is fully revealed to the wise *that* which transcends the senses and the mind, which is uncaused, which is undefinable, which has neither eyes nor ears, neither hands

> nor feet, which is all-pervading, subtler than the subtlest — the everlasting, the source of all. — *Muṇḍaka* I.i.4-6

Śaṅkara refers to the lower knowledge and truth as *vyāvahārika satya* and the higher knowledge and truth as *pāramārthika satya.* Lower knowledge and truth is conventional, relative, conditioned, practical, and mundane, whereas the higher knowledge and truth is absolute, unconditioned, and supramundane. It is clear that lower knowledge is the product of the senses and intellect, that is, knowledge obtained through superimposition; in short, lower knowledge is categorial and pertains to the changing world of phenomena. It is necessarily governed by the subject-object distinction. With respect to lower knowledge, one can always ask, "Who is the knower, what is the known, and what is the act of knowing?" All lower knowledge is thus propositional knowledge, constructed through names and forms; in brief, lower knowledge is knowledge of the world of appearances, the realm of *māyā.*

In keen contrast, the higher knowledge, transcending the senses and intellect, is non-perceptual, non-conceptual, and hence non-propositional — non-categorial — direct, and immediate (unmediated by the senses and mind). It is the knowledge of the real, the timeless, spaceless, nameless, and formless *Brahman* (*ātman*). It is to be attained through non-dual, mystical intuition (*prajña*). The higher knowledge is neither subjective nor objective, and therefore transcends the tripartite distinction of the knower, the known, and the activity of knowing, characteristic of all categorial knowledge. A moment's reflection reveals that the Upaniṣadic sages, by distinguishing higher and lower truths, were long ago familiar with the distinction between the sacred and the secular.

It is easy to see now why understanding the nature of categorial knowledge in general is necessary for understanding the higher knowledge, knowledge of the ultimate non-dual reality (*Brahman, ātman*).

What happens if someone makes an absolute claim on behalf of a categorial (lower) truth? It can be shown that, by using the categories, principles, and rules accepted by the advocate himself, such a claim *necessarily* leads to contradiction and absurdity; and since the advocate of the claim himself accepts freedom from contradiction as a necessary condition for a claim to be accepted as truth, the thinker has now to withdraw his claim. But, one might ask, what drives a thinker in the first place to make absolute claims on behalf of a categorial truth? It is ignorance of the nature of categorial truths and *attachment* to one's own categorial framework that drive the thinker to lay absolute claims on behalf of a categorial truth. One feels secure and assured insofar as one's framework is safe and secure; and any attack on one's framework is deemed as an attack on oneself. In this manner, ignorance gives rise to blindness, dogmatism, intolerance, and fanaticism, which in turn produce pain and suffering (*duḥkha*). Thus it is attachment, born out of ignorance, that brings one pain and suffering. Only by commanding insight into the nature of categorial frameworks and categorial truths does one free oneself from attachment and therewith pain and suffering.

Let me now illustrate the above observation that any absolute claim on behalf of a categorial truth leads to contradiction and absurdity. Thus, certain Western philosophers, generally known as "idealists," claim that ultimate reality is of the nature of mind. An Upaniṣadic sage will ask, "How does one first come to understand what "mind" means?" And he will go on to point out that one's understanding of "mind" is based on one's experience of non-mind, say matter; that is, if one has no experience of non-mind, then the term "mind" cannot have any meaning. In brief, we understand "mind" through our understanding of "non-mind" and vice versa. This means that "mind" and "non-mind" acquire their meanings through mutual contrast given in our experience; that is, neither of these terms can have any meaning of its own and hence their meanings are mutually dependent. Where there is no such mutual contrast, there can be no talk of any term having any meaning. Since ultimate reality is that besides which nothing can exist, no contrast is possible in regard to ultimate reality. Therefore it is absurd to characterize the ultimate non-dual reality either as mind or non-mind (matter) or, for that matter, as anything at all. In advancing an absolute claim on behalf of a categorial knowledge-claim, the philosopher takes a term which has a clear meaning within a categorial framework and tries to extend its meaning beyond and outside of the categorial framework, without realizing that the term has no meaning outside of the framework. Hence the absurdity and contradiction. Put explicitly, such an absolute claim implies ultimate reality is at once non-dual and dual. To take another example, if all objects in the universe are of the same colour, then there cannot be any difference in meaning between "red" and "blue." One can call the colour by whatever name one wants. Colour-terms have meanings because of our experience of different colours, just as "mind" and "matter" have meanings because of our experience of mind and non-mind. The insight here is that words can have meanings and referents (what they refer to) only in a domain of plurality — the world of phenomena, appearances, of the senses and the intellect — but not with regard to the non-dual reality transcending all distinctions and plurality. This is precisely what the Upaniṣadic *ṛṣi* means when he teaches that *Brahman* (*atman*) is imperceivable, inconceivable, indefinable, and inexpressible.

It is worth noting in this context that there are *many* lower truths, whereas there can only be *one* higher truth. There are many lower truths because there are many phenomena and categorial frameworks, and there is just the non-dual reality, besides which nothing can be. Every lower truth is a categorial truth, arising in and certifiable through perceptual-conceptual inquiries, methods, and procedures. Further, in the case of every lower truth, truth and being (that which makes it truth) are separable. Consider, for example, the claim that a certain planet has two satellites. This claim will be regarded as true provided there exists a certain *state of affairs* (*being*); the truth of the claim and the state of affairs that makes the claim true are clearly separable. However, in the case of the higher truth, no such separation is possible. The reason for this is that, unlike lower truths, the higher truth cannot be captured through percepts and concepts — categorial frameworks; quite to the contrary, the higher truth can only be experienced in direct, immediate, non-perceptual and non-conceptual, non-dual intuition — *prajñā.* This is so because, in the case of the higher truth, truth and being are *non-different, one and the same.* It is not as though there is truth on the one hand and its certification through a *state of affairs* on the other. Hence truth and being (*sat,* existence) are one and the same. Put another way, the higher truth cannot be apprehended as an *object* of consciousness; in coming to know the higher truth, the tripartite distinction characteristic of *every* lower truth, namely, the distinction of the knower, the known, and the activity of knowing, simply vanishes away. This is precisely what is meant by saying that in regard to the higher truth (*pāramārthika satya*), one's being *is* the truth, one's being *is* the reality, *ātman, Brahman.* Thus, in the experience of the higher truth, there can be neither propositions nor state of affairs bestowing truth upon propositions. In a word, the higher truth transcends the senses and the intellect — percepts and concepts, forms and names. The point of all these observations is that insight into the nature of categorial knowledge *points to* the higher truth — the ultimate, transcendent reality — the direct experience of which is sought by everyone in quest of knowledge, wisdom, freedom, peace, and joy. Seekers of the knowledge of the ultimate, non-dual reality are often referred to as "mystics," whether in the Western or non-Western traditions. The Upaniṣadic sages are mystics, *par excellence,* unsurpassed and unsurpassable. One might want to ask whether the Upaniṣadic *ṛṣi*s are philosophers or religious seekers. The answer is that they are at once profound philosophers and supreme religious seekers (the term *mystic* is to be understood here in the sense of one who transcends the senses and the intellect and therewith all categorial frameworks, in quest of the non-dual reality).

We shall bring this chapter to a close by making a few salient observations. One might ask, "Why did the non-dual reality (*Brahman*) become many?" Let us immediately point out that this question implies that *Brahman becomes* many; becoming takes place in time, but since *Brahman* is timeless it is a grave error to think that *Brahman* becomes many. Properly formulated, the question should be, "Why does the non-dual *Brahman* appear to us as many?" *Brahman* appears to us as many under our superimpositional activities, as has already been clarified. *Brahman* (*ātman*), being timeless, cannot be thought of as agents, doers. *Brahman* is simply *sat* (Existence) and *ātman* is pure, objectless consciousness. Have you ever seen consciousness doing anything? Consciousness (*ātman*), being timeless, does not do anything. It is merely present, the silent witness. Still, one might wonder as to why there is a world? The existence of the world cannot be explained. We should humbly and honestly admit that we do not know why there is a world at all. In fact, Śaṅkara tells us that the existence of the world is indefinable and inexplicable (*anirvacanīya*). The reason for this is as follows: argument, proof, explanation, demonstration, etc. all belong in and are applicable to the domain of plurality and variety — phenomena. There are premises and conclusion, proof and the proven (what is proved), demonstration and that which is demonstrated, explanation and that which is explained (known in philosophy of science as, "explanans" and "explanandum," respectively), and that this is so, is precisely the import of the remark that all these pertain to and govern the world of phenomena. Since the world of phenomena, having no existence (being) of its own, is non-different from *Brahman*, of which it is merely a variety of appearances, to ask as to why there is a world is to ask as to why there is *Brahman*; and since there can be nothing other than *Brahman*, to serve as an explanation of the fact that *Brahman* is, the question cannot in principle be answered. In short, the transcendent and the timeless *Brahman* (*ātman*) cannot be grasped by any *instrument*, sensory or intellectual, since the concept of instrument implies a plurality — the instrument, the task to be accomplished, and the agent operating (handling) the instrument. What does all this mean?

It means that the question as to why there is a world cannot, in principle, be answered. But, interestingly enough, the question simply vanishes away on the direct and authentic realization of *Brahman;* for in the experience of realization of *Brahman,* there can be no duality, no distinctions, not even the subject-object distinction. This question simply disappears, for the necessary conditions for its being raised, the domain of plurality and appearances, is no longer there. Remember the illustration of the magician's trick? The spectators are taken in, amazed, puzzled, and wondered as to how the magician produced a pigeon out of an allegedly empty hat. The magician himself is not surprised, puzzled, and taken in, unlike the spectators. Reason? He is the master of the trick and knows how dextrously and skilfully to produce the illusion in the spectators. But when one studies under a great magician and becomes a great magician in his own right, one is no longer surprised. In the same manner, the question as to why there is a world at all cannot be answered by any means available *within* the world of plurality. The realization of *Brahman* (*ātman*) results in the total disappearance of the question as well as the one raising the question. Rational-scientific thought cannot, therefore, in principle, explain and answer as to how and why there is a world at all. Let us illustrate this point with regard to science, as we understand and practise. Science cannot, in principle, explain the world *as a whole.* For in order to explain how the world came to be, one needs to know the conditions and circumstances (if one is permitted to talk in this way at all) *prior* to the world's coming to be; and there seems to be no way in which one can gain knowledge of these conditions and circumstances, if at all there were any. But the fact that there is a world at all forces us to acknowledge a transcendent reality — reality that transcends capture by science (categorial frameworks).

Consider the so-called Big-Bang theory. According to this theory, there originally was a singularity, a primordial black hole, with whose explosion came into being space, time, and matter. It is of no inconsiderable interest to note that one of the Indian systems of philosophy, the Sāṁkhya, gave an account of the evolution of unmanifest *prakṛti* into the world of space, time, and matter. But the question is: "What caused the Big-Bang?" There can, in principle, be no answer to this question; for, as we earlier pointed out, in order to answer this question, one needs to know the conditions and circumstances prior to the Big-Bang (known in physics as "initial conditions"). But science itself tells us that all our concepts, principles, and laws of space, time, and matter break down within (!) the singularity and therefore we cannot know what caused the Big-Bang. Scientists can only offer interesting suggestions and conjectures; and the most interesting conjecture is that the Big-Bang was caused by *spontaneous* quantum fluctuations. But does this really answer the question? Some scientists offer cosmologies of ever-expanding universe, others of steady-state universe, and yet others of an oscillating universe, Big-Bang followed by a Big Crunch, and so on. Let us also note that cosmology is not and cannot be a science, as understood and practised. Any branch of knowledge regarded as science will have *laws,* and cosmology cannot, in principle, have any laws, because laws are formulated by systematically studying reproducible (repeatable) phenomena. Since the world as a whole is not a reproducible phenomenon, cosmology, understood as the science concerned with explaining as to how and why there is a world, cannot have any laws. Nevertheless, scientists, in the light of and on the basis of astronomical observations and calculations, make conjectures as to how the world came to be; and these conjectures sometimes lead to fruitful inquiries into and understanding of astronomical phenomena. The point of all these observations, then, is that cosmology in the last analysis becomes a matter for speculation — in a word, metaphysics.

A note about lower truths and the higher truth: the distinction between lower truths and the higher truth, long ago made in the *Muṇḍaka Upaniṣad,* is none other than the distinction between the secular and the sacred; confounding lower truths with the higher truth is a product of ignorance (*avidyā*) and has grave and disastrous consequences. Lower truths pertain to the world of the senses and intellect, whereas the higher truth pertains to the transcendent non-dual reality. Thus all rational-scientific truths (all perceptual-conceptual, categorial truths, including the sciences, ethics, codes of conduct, statecraft, etc.) are lower truths. In the light of this profound insight, Indian tradition divides philosophy into two categories: philosophies of time and philosophies of eternity. The former are concerned with phenomena and hence affairs of the world of senses and intellect, whereas the latter are concerned with the eternal (timeless) transcendent non-dual reality. Accordingly, philosophies dealing with time-bound existence are known in the Indian tradition as Dharmaśāstras, philosophies of time, whereas those dealing with the transcendent non-dual reality are known as Śruti, philosophies of eternity. It is but natural, then, that philosophies of time (Dharmaśāstras) are subject to change, revision, modification, and sometimes outright rejection and replacement, whereas the Upaniṣads, dealing with the timeless non-dual reality, are not subject to change, revision, and modification. Dharmaśāstras — philosophies of time — are formulated to serve our well-being under varying conditions and circumstances; and when circumstances change and the currently existing Dharmaśāstras are no longer conducive to our well-being, we are entitled to change them, in order to serve us best. In keen contrast, the Upaniṣads, philosophies of eternity, transcending any and all time-bound existence, are not subject to any change, revision, and modification. In short, there cannot, in principle, be any such thing as a *revised* version of the Upaniṣads. There may be different *interpretations* of the Upaniṣads at different times by different people, but the Upaniṣads themselves remain the same, having at the very core of their teaching unqualified and uncompromising non-duality, entirely grounded in the most profound intuition and extraordinary intellect. Let us now illustrate the distinction between lower truths and the higher truth. Consider the following: can one charge interest on money lent? when is it appropriate to give a divorce and dissolve a marriage? what punishment is to be given for a crime, for example, murder or theft? when is abortion permissible? when is euthanasia allowable? can a person, out of religious conviction, undertake fast unto death? and so on, are all matters pertaining to the world of our senses and intellect. Answers to these questions are provided by the Dharmaśāstras, not by the philosophies of eternity. However, in the Western tradition, the answers to these questions as well as how to attain salvation are put between the two covers of the *same* book(s), the scriptures (think of the Ten Commandments). It was forbidden by the Bible to charge interest on money lent — laws against usury — and it is only by fighting many uphill battles against religious authorities that the West had freed itself from the above restrictions.

Scriptures are concerned with salvatory knowledge — the higher truth — not with the affairs of the world; yes, scriptures may give broad outlines of ethics and codes of conduct but not detailed rules and specific restrictions as to how to go about the domain of lower truths, the domain whose hallmark is change. The Vedic (Upaniṣadic) tradition is unique for never confounding the higher and lower truths. Yes, there have always been some self-proclaimed followers of the Upaniṣads who mistakenly regard the Dharmaśāstras as philosophies of eternity and thereby elevate lower, conventional truths to the status of the higher truth. Such confounding, needless to mention, can only result in attitude, conduct, and behaviour inconducive to general well-being, since conventional distinctions and categories, such as nationality, race, stock, caste, gender, occupation, etc. become rigidified and contribute to social disharmony and human ill-being.

Let it be emphasized that the distinction between lower truths and the higher truth is made in the lower truths, not in the higher truth, for the higher truth, transcending the senses and mind, is devoid of any and all distinctions, including the one between the higher truth and lower truths.

A brief explanation of Dharmaśāstras: the term *dharma* comes from the Sanskrit root√*dhṛ*, meaning to support, to maintain, to sustain, to uphold, etc. *Dharma* is that which supports, maintains, and sustains societies, human as well as non-human. *Dharma* cannot be translated into English in a simple and straightforward manner; we can only give a cluster of meanings, such as truth; justice; that which is appropriate, fitting, and fair; duties; rights; obligations, and so on. *Śāstra* means science (any systematic body of knowledge); thus Dharmaśāstra means the science of all those things that are necessary for the protection and preservation of societies. Some people who have turned to vegetarianism have tried to make their pet cats and dogs also vegetarians, by offering them carrots, cabbage, and rice; this is clearly misguided, for it is the *dharma* of cats and dogs to consume and sustain themselves on non-vegetarian foods. Does a herd of elephants have a *dharma?* Does a pride of lions have a *dharma?* Does a colony of chimpanzees have a *dharma?* Does a colony of ants or bees have a *dharma?* The answer to all these questions is clearly in the affirmative, for wherever there are societies, there is *dharma,* which means that wherever there is no *dharma,* there can be no societies, human or non-human.

5

Religious Significance

In this chapter, I shall systematically discuss the implications of non-duality (*advaita*) and their significance to the religious quest. This discussion will naturally (inevitably) lead us to an examination and analysis of mysticism, at the very heart of the religious quest, whether Western or non-Western.

When we survey the history of religions, we notice that it is full of dogmatism, exclusiveness, intolerance, fanaticism, violence, and unspeakable horrors and cruelty. This is more so in the history of Western religions than that of non-Western religions, in particular the Indian and the Chinese. What is the reason for this sad and tragic state of affairs? In the light of our discussion of categorial (perceptual-conceptual) frameworks and categorial knowledge, the answer should be clear and straightforward: Each group of people lays absolute claims on behalf of its own religion and condemns those of others as false and dangerous, deserving only to be eliminated. In this manner arise religious wars and forced conversions. What went wrong? One fails to realize that one's own religion is the result of a certain superimpositional activity, a categorial framework, depending upon a variety of factors such as language, geography, socio-political and economic circumstances, and so on; and one makes absolute and exclusive claims for the truth of one's own religion. Hence arise conflict and opposition, resulting in wars and the attendant pain and suffering. In other words, religious conflict is a direct consequence of ignorance (*avidyā*) of the nature of categorial knowledge. Thus knowledge of the nature of categorial knowledge in general liberates one from the shackles of attachment, dogmatism, exclusivism, blindness, intolerance, and fanaticism, and makes possible the pursuit and attainment of the higher truth (*pāramārthika satya*), knowledge of the non-difference of ultimate reality (*Brahman*) and one's true being (*ātman*), resulting in wisdom, freedom, peace, joy, and enhancement of the well-being of all sentient beings, here as well as elsewhere in the vast cosmos (*lokasaṁgraha*).

We have pointed out earlier that when Westerners first encounter the Upaniṣads they feel puzzled and wonder as to why the Upaniṣads are regarded as "sacred writings." The reason for this puzzlement is the fact that one rarely comes across in the Upaniṣads any discussion of God; instead, one finds in the Upaniṣads discussions of ultimate reality, one's true being, and the nature and status of the world (of phenomena). Put pointedly, Western religious discourse revolves around God whereas the Upaniṣadic discourse revolves around ultimate reality. As such, Westerners wonder why the Upaniṣads are regarded as religious works at all. Yes, there certainly is discourse on God, especially in the *Śvetāśvatara Upaniṣad.* However, God here is to be understood in the overall context — the main drift and thrust — of the Upaniṣadic teaching, thoroughgoing non-dualism. God is not denied, and the existence and nature of God is lucidly articulated and clarified. I shall now turn to a discussion of God in the Upaniṣadic teaching.

Consistent with the distinction between lower truths and the higher truth — perceptual-conceptual truths on the one hand and the non-perceptual and non-conceptual truth on the other, to be realized directly, immediately, and intuitively, respectively known as *vyāvahārika satya* and *pāramārthika satya* — the Upaniṣads distinguish between *Brahman* conceived of as having form, name, qualities, and relations, and *Brahman,* conceived of as formless, nameless, and wholly devoid of qualities and relations, respectively known as *Saguṇa Brahman* and *Nirguṇa Brahman. Brahman* (*ātman*), the ultimate non-dual reality, being formless and nameless, cannot, in principle be conceived of; however, human beings, being frail and feeble, nevertheless try to conceive of the inconceivable, and thereby give a form, name, qualities, and relations to the inconceivable *Brahman*. *Brahman* so conceived of is God (*Īśvara*), as understood in *all* theistic traditions, Western and non-Western alike. It is obvious that such a conception belongs to the lower, conventional, relative, conditioned, practical standpoint; whereas the inconceivable *Brahman*, devoid of form, name, qualities, and relations, belongs to the higher, absolute standpoint. *Saguṇa Brahman* is God (*Īśvara*), understood as the cause, creator, sustainer, destroyer, and judge of the world. It is *Saguṇa Brahman* that people worship in different forms and names, such as Rāma, Kr̥ṣṇa, Śiva, Jesus, Allah, Jehovah, and so on. It is God as the *Saguṇa Brahman* that is endowed with such qualities as love, kindness, and mercy. It is *Saguṇa Brahman* (God) who stands in relation to the world. In short, *Saguṇa Brahman* is *personal* God. But since form, name, qualities, and relations can only belong in the realm of appearances (phenomena), *Saguṇa Brahman* (God) is an appearance, although the highest among appearances, and not reality. On the other hand, *Nirguṇa Brahman*, being reality beyond names and forms, is neither the cause nor the creator nor the sustainer nor the destroyer of the world. *Nirguṇa Brahman* can be neither worshipped nor prayed to. *Nirguṇa Brahman* is the non-dual reality, non-different from *ātman* (pure consciousness, one's true being). The above observations make it abundantly clear that different theistic religious traditions are the result of different *conceptions* of the *inconceivable* ultimate non-dual reality (*Brahman, ātman*). God is thus a concept, an image, a projection; each theistic religion has its own conception and image of the inconceivable *Brahman*. The adherents of each theistic religion, being ignorant of the fact that the God of their own religion is merely a concept and image of the inconceivable ultimate non-dual reality, go on to claim that only their God is the true God and the god(s) of other religions are false gods. In this manner arise conflict and opposition, and each group of people tries to convert other peoples to its own religion, and such attempts necessarily lead to religious animosity, forced conversions, and unspeakable violence and cruelty, all, strangely enough, in the name of their god(s) (simply think of the Crusades, you will see the point). Does this mean that God is unreal? Certainly not; God is the highest among appearances (phenomena) and we have clarified earlier that appearance is *not* unreality (unreality cannot, in principle, be an appearance, a phenomenon). Yes, there are different conceptions of the inconceivable *Brahman* and each conception is the basis of a certain theistic religion; and to each conception there corresponds an appearance (only an appearance), and appearances are *not* unreal. Like all other phenomena, God (*Īśvara*) is neither real nor unreal. God is not real, insofar as it is an appearance (phenomenon); nor is God unreal, because the unreal can never, in principle, be experienced. The God of every theistic religion is an *appearance* of *Brahman* — the non-dual reality — and there is a clear and undeniable distinction between appearance and reality. There is the non-dual reality and there are many *appearances* of it in different theistic traditions; and no one should mistake appearances for reality, although there cannot be any appearances without a reality. (Remember the example where John X, the actor, appears on the stage one day as Alexander, another day as Caesar, and yet on another day as Napoleon, and no matter how many times you see John X's performances, you never come to know John X himself but only his appearances?). Just so, knowing God is not knowing *Brahman,* the non-dual, ultimate reality, of which it (God) is merely an appearance.

It may be pointed out here that there is a parallel between the individual self (*jīva*) and *Saguṇa Brahman* (God) on the one hand and between *ātman* and *Nirguṇa Brahman* on the other. Both the individual ego and *Saguṇa Brahman* are products of *māyā,* of superimpositional activity, whereas both *ātman* and *Nirguṇa Brahman* are beyond *māyā,* beyond perceptions and conceptions. Just as *ātman* appears as the individual ego under the limitations of body and mind, so also *Nirguṇa Brahman* appears as *Saguṇa Brahman* (God) owing to cosmic ignorance, and therewith the superimpositional activities. The chief and only goal of the Upaniṣadic teaching is to realize the non-dual reality (*ātman, Brahman*) and to never settle for appearances, no matter how lofty, exalted, and sublime.

It is obvious that it is only with respect to *Saguṇa Brahman* (God) that one can talk about the being that is omnipotent (all-powerful), omniscient (all-knowing), omni-benevolent (all-good), and the creator of the world, and, accordingly, hold him responsible for the good and evil in the world of appearances. In stark contrast, *Nirguṇa Brahman,* being the sole reality, is beyond good and evil, which are exclusively confined to the world of phenomena (appearances), of plurality, variety, and multiplicity — in a word, time-bound existence. *Brahman,* the non-dual reality, is timeless and therefore transcends all dualities, including that of good and evil. The *advaitin* recognizes the need for the concept of *Saguṇa Brahman* (God, *Īśvara*) as engendering genuine religious consciousness in as yet unenlightened human beings. It is conducive to the cultivation of moral virtues and piety, such as truthfulness, charity, kindness, compassion, humility, self-sacrifice, and so on. *Saguṇa Brahman* therefore serves as the stepping-stone in one's striving for knowledge of ultimate reality and therewith one's true being. However, the *advaitin* emphatically maintains, in the true and uncompromising spirit of the Upaniṣadic teaching, that knowledge of ultimate reality cannot be attained unless one transcends *all* conceptions and images — *Saguṇa Brahman.* Only knowledge of *Nirguṇa Brahman* is knowledge of the ultimate non-dual reality — liberating knowledge. I shall now turn to a discussion of bondage and freedom in the Upaniṣadic teaching. On doing this, I shall go on to clarify the problem of plurality of religious traditions and show that unity among different religions cannot, in principle, be sought at the level of conceptions, images, projections, and doctrines but only at the mystical level, transcending all concepts, images, and doctrines — in a word, at the trans-perceptual-conceptual level, that of direct, immediate (un-mediated by senses and mind), non-dual intuition (*prajñā*). I shall further show that all *truly* mystical traditions, whether Western or non-Western, lead to the same realization, the realization of the unity of *all* existence and the non-difference of ultimate reality (*Brahman*) and one's true being (*ātman*); in short, to the affirmation of a reality that is non-dual (transcending the subject-object distinction, hence transcending the senses and the mind).

According to the Upaniṣadic teaching, the human being's state of bondage and suffering is due not to any original sin but to original ignorance (*avidyā*). It is by conquering this ignorance by the knowledge of reality — of the non-difference of *ātman* and *Brahman* — that one attains *mokṣa,* the state of absolute freedom from ignorance, *māyā,* bondage, and suffering. For this reason, knowledge of reality is called "liberating knowledge." It is also called "soteriological knowledge," in that it radically transforms the human being. One who has attained *mokṣa* is freed once and for all from ignorance, illusion, delusion, attachment, and fear, including fear of death. By overcoming ignorance by the knowledge of the real, one has brought the kārmic chain to an end and thereby has broken out of the circle of births and deaths. One has thus gone beyond birth and death and attained immortality. It should be emphasized that "immortality" is not to be understood as endless existence in some distant and unknown world. Rather, it means that one has discovered that birth and death are products of *māyā* and ignorance confined to the world of appearances and that in one's true being one is infinite and eternal, untouched by birth and death. *Mokṣa,* absolute freedom, is not a state to be looked forward to after death. On the contrary, *mokṣa* is the attainment of the knowledge of the non-difference *of ātman* and *Brahman,* to be attained *here and now,* while fully embodied. He who so attains *mokṣa* is known as *jīvanmukta* the living-free. At death, he attains *videhamukti,* the final and absolute freedom from all fetters of *māyā.* To attain *mokṣa* is to attain knowledge of one's true being as the ultimate non-dual reality that permeates all existence. The "liberated" man (attainer of *mokṣa*) is thus one who has overcome all the distinctions and oppositions that plague men in ignorance and bondage. In particular, he has overcome the nightmare of ignorant philosophies — the opposition between freedom and necessity and good and evil. Having attained knowledge of the real, one has overcome all forms of alienation, alienation from the world, from others, and from oneself. *Mokṣa*, then, is the state of self-knowledge, wisdom, freedom, peace, and joy. The mokshic person thus lives a life of spontaneity. In brief, the mokshic person is the very embodiment and exemplar of *sat* (Pure Existence), *cit* (Pure Consciousness), and *ānanda* (Pure Bliss).

Although the *advaitin* himself prefers and recommends *jñāna-yoga*, characterized as intellectual-spiritual discipline (or simply put, the way of knowledge), as the means to attain *mokṣa*, he also recognizes other *yoga*s as appropriate and adequate means for the realization of ultimate reality. I shall now proceed to discuss the four *yoga*s (paths).

Let us first note that the Upaniṣadic tradition, unlike all other traditions, emphasizes that, insofar as human beings differ from each other, different types of persons find different paths appropriate and efficacious to them. Accordingly, the tradition formulated four different paths (*yoga*s) for the realization of ultimate reality, variously known as *Brahman*, *ātman*, "The That," and so on. These paths are: *bhakti-yoga*, *karma-yoga*, *jñāna-yoga*, and *rāja-yoga*: Each of these paths is best suited to human beings of a certain type. To prescribe a single path to all people is like a physician's prescribing one and the same medication to people suffering from different kinds of ailment and disease (what is more, a good physician prescribes different medications to different people suffering from the *same* disease, in the light of the differences in their constitutions and medical histories). The result of prescribing a single medication, whatever it may be and however kindly dispensed, is positively harmful; for, besides not curing some persons, it creates complications which may and often do lead to death. Some people may object to the claim that human beings differ from each other, by saying that it is undemocratic, elitist, provincial, and even racist. I should at once point out that such an objection is not based on any facts but is merely the reaction of blind and uncritical commitment to a *mistaken* conception of egalitarianism. What is the mistaken conception of egalitarianism I speak of? Genuine egalitarianism is based, paradoxical as it might seem, on the recognition of the fact that human beings are different from each other. The true spirit of egalitarianism may be expressed as follows: human beings are, as a matter of fact, different from one another, but this fact should not be taken as justification for treating certain peoples and persons disrespectfully, inconsiderately, and inhumanely; on the contrary, *despite* their differences, which are many and varied, all human beings, simply by virtue of the fact that they are human beings, are entitled to equality of respect, dignity, consideration, opportunity, and to equality before the law. The heart of true and authentic egalitarianism, then, is this commitment towards all human beings, irrespective of differences, but not the denial of their differences, whatever the reasons for the differences. It is the denial of the differences that I call "mistaken conception of egalitarianism." It is clear that the recognition of differences among human beings is presupposed by true and genuine egalitarianism. For is it not the case that, were all human beings the same and alike, much as the products emerging from an assembly line, there would be no need for egalitarianism at all? To put it differently, where there are no differences, there is no need for egalitarianism.

It is an undeniable fact of observation that human beings differ from one another in many respects — physical, mental, and emotional — whatever the reasons for the differences. Thus some people are predominantly intellectual, reflective, and contemplative; others, emotional (feeling-oriented), and hence aesthetically and artistically inclined; yet others, mechanically inclined and pragmatic; still others, religious, and so on. For our purposes, the reasons as to why human beings are different from each other are irrelevant. That is, we start out by simply acknowledging the fact that human beings are different from one another and then ask, in the light of this fact, whether it makes sense to think that there is a *single* path for *all* human beings. The answer is clearly in the negative. Consider, as an example, the following case: a man wants to go from New York to San Francisco. Suppose we gave him the map of an air-route. This map will serve him well only if he has an aircraft. But if he has only an automobile, is it not appropriate that we supply him with a road-map? On the other hand, if he has a yacht and wishes to travel by it, neither of the earlier maps will be useful to him; instead, he needs a map of a water-route. Just as people with different modes of transportation need different kinds of maps to get from where they are to their destination(s), so also human beings with different physical, mental, emotional make up — kārmic baggages — need different routes and hence different maps — *means* and *paths* — in order to arrive at the *same* destination, the existential, authentic realization and thereby certification of the non-difference of ultimate reality (*Brahman*) and one's true being (*ātman*). Hence different paths.

BHAKTI-YOGA (THE PATH OF DEVOTION)

This path is best suited to those who are predominantly of a devotional turn of personality (*bhakti,* devotion). These are people who are not much concerned with intellectual inquiry; rather, they are persons capable of unshakable and rocklike faith in and devotion to God (of course in their chosen form, whether Jehovah, Jesus, Allah, Kr̥ṣṇa, Rāma, Śiva, The Great Spirit — of the Amerindians — the Great Mother, Durgā, Kālī, and so on). Cultivation of unsurpassed and unsurpassable humility, love, charity, and total non-aggression, constant remembrance of God are the heart of this path. Through self-surrender to God, the devotee (*bhakta*) eventually succeeds in emptying the ego and on such emptying arises direct experience and knowledge of God, which is wholly devoid of any and all distinctions and dualities, including the subject-object distinction. This experience and knowledge transcends the senses and mind — percepts and concepts — and the devotee is no longer there as an ego — *subject* — to experience God as an *object, phenomenon,* and therefore the experience of God is pure consciousness (consciousness without a subject and an object). This knowledge and experience is thus through and through non-dual, in which the tripartite distinction of the knower, the known, and the act of knowing, characteristic of all knowing through the senses and the mind, simply vanishes away. Hence the Upaniṣadic proclamation, "I am *Brahman* (*ātman*). More will be said about this non-dual experience and knowledge in the sequel, in our discussion of mysticism and mystical experience. It is a common error among the more cerebral people to think that the path of devotion is an easy path. Nothing, however, could be farther from the truth. The path of devotion, as explained here, is as arduous and demanding as any of the other three paths. In order to appreciate how difficult this path is, simply think of what the path demands: freedom from the assault of doubt (concerning the existence of God), total, complete, and absolute submission to God, constant remembrance of God, and thereby emptying the ego — killing the ego. To the devotee, the existence of God is not just a matter of belief and intellectual (theoretical) demonstration; instead, for him, if anything is certain, and absolutely certain, it is the existence of God, the Lord and Master of all existence, what was, is, and will be. Further, for the devotee, in the light of his total surrender to God — *prapatti* — everything that happens, happens because it is pleasing to God: "Who am I to complain? Who am I to tell Him I am hungry and in need of food? Does He (She) not know? Is there anything that is hidden from Him (Her)? Food comes to me when God is pleased; if it pleases God that I go without food, I go without food and I am nobody to complain, gripe, and grumble." This is not to say, however, that one who treads the path of devotion should not work and make an honest living. The point is rather that for the devotee his efforts and successes as well as failures are all God's will and pleasure. Thus he does not feel proud and boastful when he is successful and prosperous or feel frustrated and blame others or God when he fails. For the devotee, he is himself a nobody, a nothing, while God is everything, the Lord of all that happens and does not happen. It is to be stressed that this attitude on the part of the devotee is not to be confused with fatalism; for at the very core of the devotional path is God, who is to be served with utter devotion. There is no room in this path for hopelessness, anguish, nihilism, etc. since the devotee is fully anchored in God. There is no such anchoring to the fatalist and he is therefore open to the onslaughts of doubt, despair, nihilism, and hopelessness. The devotee is ever free, peaceful, loving, humble, and joyful; for he has placed himself in the hands of the most high, whom none can touch but who touches everything. It should be clear by now that the devotional path is as hard and exacting as any other. If you are still unconvinced, try to attain freedom from doubt and cultivate humility and surrender yourself absolutely and unconditionally to God; you will see how tough the devotional path is.

KARMA-YOGA (THE PATH OF ACTION)

This path is best suited for those people who are essentially of an active nature, the doers. That is, it serves best those who are predominantly activity-oriented, in contrast with, for example, those who are relatively passive, reflective, and contemplative. The path of action, then, is for those who, through their committed and active involvement in the affairs of the world, seek to attain the experience and knowledge of ultimate reality. Thus at the heart of the path of action lie total commitment and dedication to actively working for the well-being of the world (*lokasaṁgraha*). It is of the highest importance to clarify here the term "action." "Action," in the context of *karma-yoga* means action without attachment to the fruits and consequences of the action, for it is not the action but one's attachment to the consequences — fruits — of the action that brings one pain and suffering. It is quite difficult for people in general, and Westerners in particular, to understand as to why in the first place one acts if one does not have any attachment to the fruits and consequences of the action. This question and the wonderment therewith are a direct consequence of a grave failure to distinguish attachment from *concern.* Consider the following example, not uncommon at all: A young woman delivers a baby and she does not have the means and facilities needed for the care of the baby, such as shelter, food, clothing, medical assistance, and of course love and attention. Now someone who is a caring and loving person, also quite wealthy, comes forward and says, "Please give the baby to me and I will take good care, and, what is more, you can always come and visit and even take the baby with you for weekends." We have always known, as a matter of fact, that the young woman will be quite reluctant to part with the baby. Reason? She knows she is in no position to take care of the baby and yet she refuses to offer the baby where full caring, love, and attention are available and promised. There is, on the part of the young mother, attachment, which she confuses with *concern;* if she is concerned about the well-being of the baby, she should offer the baby for adoption, under the best circumstances and conditions. I hope that the distinction between attachment and concern is hereby clarified. To take another example, consider the following. One of our friends or relatives is seriously ill; what is it that we should do? We should do everything in our power and at our disposal in order to alleviate his pain and suffering and restore his health. But if after our best efforts, the person dies, there is no point in our crying and feeling bad; for no good comes out of our crying either for the person who died or for us. The fact that one does not cry does not mean that one lacks love, care, and compassion towards the dead person; rather, it means that one understands the nature of things and that death is but a natural and inevitable fact of life. The truth of the matter is that when people gather around a dead person and cry, they really cry for themselves, and they cry out of attachment to the dead person. One will be truly concerned for the dead person, if one is of help, assistance, and encouragement to the dead person's family and dependents.

Thus only actions performed without attachment constitute *karma-yoga.* Actions performed with attachment are grounded in ignorance and unfreedom; and since the goal of *karma-yoga,* like that of the other three *yoga*s, is knowledge of ultimate reality and therewith wisdom, freedom, peace, and joy, actions performed with attachment are incompatible with *karma-yoga.* The underlying insight here is that attachment is born of egoism, of one form or another; therefore, actions done with attachment are selfishly motivated actions, no matter how subtly veiled such motivation. It is only actions purified of every vestige of selfishness that are truly actions without attachment. One performs actions which, in the light of one's best knowledge and belief, are appropriate under a given set of circumstances but is not concerned with the success or failure of the actions or the fruits thereof; for to be so concerned is precisely what it is to be attached. It is of the utmost importance to note that it is not performing or not performing an action that is the cause of pain, sorrow, and suffering; rather, it is the attitude one has towards the consequences (fruits) of acting or not acting. Thus if a student studies a subject well — with the aim of attaining understanding and mastery — and takes an examination and for some reason does not do well and receives only a moderate grade and feels bad about it, it is clear that his pain and unhappiness are brought about by his *attitude* towards the *result*s (fruits) of his taking the examination, but not by his taking the examination. *Karma-yoga* exhorts human beings to perform actions to the best of their abilities and facilities and not grieve over the consequences of the actions. Action without attachment, then, is action untainted by egoism and selfishness. Great social and political reformers and others who unremittingly work for the enhancement of the well-being of the world are *karma-yogin*s in varying degrees. The follower of the path of action is further exhorted to dedicate every one of his actions as an offering to God (in his chosen form). Now ask: What kind of things does one offer God? Is it not true that only the best at one's disposal is worthy of offering to God? What is meant by "best" here? By "best" is meant everything pure and of the highest value. It is clear that every action the follower of the path of action performs must be pure — in the sense of non-egoistic, unselfish, and unattached — in order for it to qualify to be a fitting offering to God.

One might now ask: Does it mean, then, that the follower of *karma-yoga* must be a theist? No, it means nothing of the kind. If one is a theist, one's actions are looked upon as offerings to God; but the emphasis here is on non-attachment and purity of action, not on one's being a theist or atheist. That one is an avowed atheist does not mean that one cannot perform actions without attachment. The main thrust of *karma-yoga* is that through dedication to serving the world by pure, unselfish, and unattached action even the atheist attains experience and knowledge of ultimate reality. We may note again that *karma-yoga,* like *bhakti-yoga* (the path of devotion), is aimed at emptying the ego, in order that one may realize ultimate reality; that is, the goal is the same, although the paths are different, each being appropriate and best suited to persons of a certain type. The *bhakti-yogin* succeeds in emptying the ego through unswerving and absolute self-surrender to God, whereas the *karma-yogin* accomplishes this same goal by cultivating utter unselfishness and by working through action without attachment for the welfare of all sentient beings. In either case, the destination is the same: experience of ultimate reality through seeing the emptiness of the ego.

It should be noted that *karma-yoga, like bhakti-yoga,* is an arduous and exacting path. If someone doubts this observation, let him strive to be unselfish and unattached and be maximally concerned for the well-being of all; he will soon see that the path of action is as difficult and demanding as any other.

RĀJA-YOGA (THE PATH OF PSYCHO-PHYSIOLOGICAL EXPLORATION)

This path is eminently suited to those people who have the inclination and ability for a long, detailed, and systematic investigation of the physiological and psychological strands of their personalities. It goes without saying that this path requires extraordinary self-discipline and great effort and concentration. *Rāja-yoga* consists of a variety of psycho-physiological exercises and techniques, by practising which one gains knowledge and control of the physiological and psychological processes — knowledge and control of the physical, mental, and emotional aspects of one's being. Pātañjali's *Yoga-Sūtras* is the classic text on *rāja-yoga,* also known as the *aṣṭāṅga-yoga,* meaning the eight-limbed *yoga*. There are, in addition, innumerable works of major and minor significance on the subject. The aim of *rāja-yoga,* like that of *bhakti-yoga* and *karma-yoga,* is experience and knowledge of ultimate reality. *Rāja-yoga* realizes this aim through experimental inquiry into the psycho-physiological make-up of the human being. For this reason, *rāja-yoga* is aptly described as the *science* of the human being. Systematic observation and mastery of a variety of states of consciousness, ordinary as well as extraordinary, is the warp and woof of *rāja-yoga.* Through the attainment of total cessation of mental activity — *cittavr̥tti nirodha* — arises the experience and knowledge of ultimate reality (*Brahman, ātman*). An accomplished *rāja-yogin* is one who has acquired total power, mastery, and control over the body-mind complex.

Experimenting with various powerful techniques such as breath-control (*prāṇāyāma*), the practitioner of *rāja-yoga* comes to command knowledge of the various facets of the constitution of the human being. He also gains knowledge of the subconscious and the unconscious and thereby of the modes of being and operation of the physical, mental, and emotional domains. Through complete mastery and control of the senses and the mind, the *rāja-yogin* comes to see the emptiness of the ego and thereby gains experience and knowledge of ultimate reality.

It may be noted again that the emptying of the ego — which is the same, clearly seeing that the ego is merely an appearance, time-bound existent — is central to *rāja-yoga,* as it is to the other two *yoga*s we have discussed, although their methods are different. The *rāja-yogin* sees the emptiness of the ego by disciplined work on himself. In order to see how difficult and demanding is *rāja-yoga,* one need only realize the chattering that incessantly goes on in one's own mind without one's being even aware of it; and if one is not aware of and in charge of one's own thoughts and emotions, in what sense can one claim to be free? Thoughts and emotions are always arising apparently without being initiated and set into motion by oneself. The main point of *rāja-yoga,* then, is that as long as one exists in this manner, one is both ignorant and unfree. But when by effort and discipline the modifications of the mind are brought to a total cessation, ultimate non-dual reality is revealed — just as the reflection of the moon is clearly seen in a *calm and unruffled* lake.

JÑĀNA-YOGA (THE PATH OF KNOWLEDGE)

The path of knowledge is for those persons who are distinguished by an inquiring mind; that is, this path serves best those who by temperament, ability, and training are inclined towards and most seriously committed to rational inquiry of the highest standards into the human being, the world, and ultimate reality. Highly developed logical-analytical intellect, coupled with the facility for keen observation and flashes of synthetic intuition — the ability to see several things or aspects of things as constituting a consistent, significant, and illuminating pattern — are essential for *jñāna-yoga.* This *yoga,* then, is for those who accept no claim unless and until every objection against it has been successfully answered and every doubt allayed. Whereas the follower of *bhakti-yoga* quells all doubts by cultivating unshakable faith in and devotion to God, the follower of *jñāna-yoga* overcomes doubt through the development and exercise of discriminative intellect (*buddhi*). For the practitioner of *jñāna-yoga,* then, mind and its activities — production of doubt and knowledge — are themselves the object of relentless scrutiny and understanding. It is by attaining such understanding through rigorous and uncompromising inquiry that the follower of *jñāna-yoga* is led to the experience and knowledge of ultimate reality. It is obvious that *jñāna-yoga* is not for the intellectually weak, timid, and lazy; rather, it is for those whose personalities are predominantly cerebral and whose commitment to *rational* inquiry is absolute and unqualified. In other words, the follower of *jñāna-yoga* is one endowed with extraordinary intellectual energy and a natural bent for reflection and contemplation.

Like the other paths, *jñāna-yoga* is a difficult and exacting path. It is true that there are many who hold in contempt persons given to intellectual inquiry in the sense of *jñāna-yoga* (remember the derogatory terms "egghead and dweller of the ivory tower"?). This negative attitude is understandable once we realize how many people find it difficult and painful to clearly think, understand, and express themselves. Just find out for yourself how rarely we really listen to someone speak. Seldom do we hear with attention, let alone understand, what the other person is saying. It is only occasionally, as interruptions of the stream of our own thoughts and emotions, that we happen to listen to someone speak. What this means, then, is that undivided attention, clarity of thought and expression, and unbiased and systematic inquiry are the heartbeats of *jñāna-yoga.*

It is through unrelenting inquiry, sustained reflection, and serene contemplation that the follower of *jñāna-yoga* is led to the knowledge of the emptiness of the ego. Seeing the emptiness of the ego is thus the goal common to all the paths; and the *jñāna-yogin* attains the goal primarily through the instrumentality of discriminative intellect. On comprehending the emptiness of the ego, there arises the experience and knowledge of the non-dual reality (*Brahman, ātman*).

It is worth noting that, although the four paths are clearly distinguishable through their salient features, it would be a mistake to think that they are therefore mutually exclusive. On the contrary, it is often the case that one and the same person practises more than one path, one of them being dominant and most suited to him. Thus any of the four paths may be primary with another as secondary, depending upon the person's temperament and inclination. It is only rarely that one pursues one of the paths to the exclusion of the others.

The prophets of the Old Testament, Jesus and the apostles of the New Testament are exclusively *bhakti-yogins*; Augustine, Aquinas, and Meister Eckhart are primarily *bhakti-yogins* and secondarily *jñāna-yogins*. Lincoln, Gandhi, Mother Teresa, and Martin Luther King, Jr. are exemplars of *bhakti* and *karma* paths. Plato and Plotinus are primarily *jñāna-yogins*; Śaṅkara, the great Advaita-Vedāntin, Nāgārjuna, the celebrated Buddhist philosopher and patriarch, and Lao Tze, the great Chinese sage, are primarily *jñāna-yogins*, and so on.

It cannot be overemphasized that for a person to follow a path not suited to him is not only not beneficial but is even harmful to him. Thus it is of the highest importance to find out what path(s) is most appropriate to oneself. Think of someone, in whom strength and courage are not dominant traits, trying to become a great warrior; before long, he will surely lose his life.

Although the Upaniṣads emphasize the path of knowledge, they clearly recognize the other paths, in the light of their insight and wisdom that no single path serves best different types of human beings. It should be clear that, although the paths are different, *knowledge of ultimate reality* is at the very heart of each of the paths. In short, experience and knowledge of ultimate reality is the goal of all the paths. It should also be clear that, although we have distinguished the four paths, in practice one usually follows two paths, one primary and the other secondary, in various combinations. Thus for someone the path of devotion may be primary and one of the other three secondary; for someone else, the path of knowledge may be primary and one of the other three secondary; and so on.

Śaṅkara, the founder of Advaita Vedānta, recommends the fourfold discipline — *sādhana-catuṣṭaya* — as a practical aid to the seeker of experience and knowledge of ultimate reality. The discipline consists of *samanyasa, śravaṇa, manana,* and *dhyāna.*

Samanyasa is the cultivation in oneself of the following qualities: (a) the ability to discriminate between the real on the one hand and appearances and the unreal on the other; the capacity to discern between the timeless and the timebound, the eternal and the transient, the infinite and the finite; (b) total indifference to both pleasure and pain under all circumstances, either here or elsewhere; renunciation of all worldly desires and attachments; (c) tranquillity, self-control, dispassion, fortitude, power of mental concentration, and faith in one's own abilities; and (d) single-minded desire for true freedom.

Śravaṇa is listening to the sages as they expound the great truths of the Upaniṣads as well as studying the various Vedāntic texts. Through *śravaṇa,* one learns the sole reality of *Brahman* and the non-difference of *Brahman* and *ātman* (That thou art). In *śravaṇa,* the role of the *guru* (teacher, master) as a living example of the liberated human being cannot be overemphasized.

Manana is the stage of reflection, in which the aspirant subjects to systematic analysis and investigation what he has learned from his *guru* and the works of the sages. He examines the teachings and weighs them in the light of reason and experience — arguments, counter-arguments, demonstrations, evidence, analogies and metaphors from everyday experience, etc. — and becomes intellectually convinced of their truth. But intellectual understanding and conviction, no matter how clear, firm, and convincing, can only provide *mediate* knowledge. Moreover, intellectual understanding and conviction are subject to change, especially under the burden of old habits of thought, resulting in the doubting and rejecting of what has hitherto been held as infallible truth. What is needed is to transform the intellectually grasped (mediate) knowledge into one's own immediate experience. The seeker therefore now undertakes *dhyāna* (yogic meditation) on the central Advaitic truth of the non-difference of *Brahman* (ultimate non-dual reality) and *ātman* (one's true being, pure consciousness). Through prolonged and intense meditation, he comes to see in a flash of non-dual intuition — *prajñā* — that he is indeed *Brahman,* the sole reality.

The question now arises: How does one experience the world, after one has attained knowledge of the non-dual reality *Brahman* (*ātman*)? We have pointed out earlier, in our discussion of the principle of two kinds of knowledge and truth, that the higher truth (*pāramārthika satya*), unlike lower truths, is soteriological, in that it radically transforms him who attains it. After the realization of the higher truth (*Brahman, ātman*), one continues to experience the world as one did prior to the realization. That is, one continues to perceive various phenomena — trees, stars, galaxies, animals (non-human as well as human), and so on, but with the most important and significant difference: Formerly one used to see them as the *other* but now one does *not* see them as the other; in short, for the realized person, there is no longer the other, there is just the *non-dual* reality (*Brahman*). One experiences the joys and sorrows of others as one's own. Gone with the sense of oneself as an individual ego are selfishness, jealousy, ill will, hatred, anger, greed, cruelty, and fear, including fear of death. For as the Upaniṣads teach, is it not true that fear can only be where there is the other? Accordingly, where there is no other, there can be no fear, either. In short, he who experiences *Brahman* sees himself in everything and everything in himself. This brings us to a discussion of mysticism and mystical experience.

I am fully aware that mysticism is a complex subject and has been dealt with through the ages by several learned men and women, in various climes and times. It is not my purpose here to undertake a historical study of mysticism, Eastern and Western (which will in itself be a treatise and hence a task for another book). Rather, my purpose here is far humbler and straightforward: to clarify mysticism and mystical experience, whether in the East or in the West. What exactly is mystical experience? What are the distinguishing traits and features of mystical experience? One can find the answers to these questions, in a single, thundering voice, with wholly unambiguous unanimity, by systematically studying the mystical works (the authors of which are themselves authentic mystics). All mystics, whether of the Western or non-Western traditions, proclaim, on the basis of their own experience — mystical experience — that there is a non-dual ultimate reality and that the non-dual reality is non-different from their own true being. In a word, a mystic is one who teaches that in one's true being one is at *unity* with the non-dual ultimate reality. A word of clarification concerning the difference between unity and union: People often synonymously use the terms "unity" and "union." But they are not synonymous and there is a vast difference between their meanings, a difference central to the understanding of mystical experience. "Union" means a collective entity, in which those which make up the union exist as individual entities. Thus, for example, the United States of America is a union of a number of states; the states do not disappear in the union but continue to exist as individually identifiable entities. In keen contrast, "unity" means total lack of any individual existence. Thus when a mystic declares that in his experience he discovered that he is at unity with the ultimate non-dual reality, he means that he and ultimate reality are indistinguishable, non-different, one and the same. It is true that mystics often try to interpret the mystical experience in terms of the concepts and ideas they inherit from their traditions. Accordingly, a mystic from a theistic tradition, while proclaiming on the one hand that his experience, transcending the subject-object distinction, is experience of the non-dual ultimate reality, nevertheless uses the term "God" to refer to the non-dual reality of his experience. How is one to understand this paradoxical situation? The answer is clear and straightforward: the mystic himself tells us that his experience, transcending the senses and the mind and hence language and thought — is truly ineffable and indescribable; all mystics, whether from theistic or non-theistic traditions, agree on the ineffability of the experience. This is the central and distinguishing characteristic of mystical experience; and it is quite understandable, then, that when a mystic talks about the untalkable (ineffable) he naturally resorts to the terminology he has inherited from his tradition.

It is for this reason that one finds different interpretations of the mystical experience as articulated by mystics from different traditions. The point of all these observations is that the heart of the mystical experience does not consist of the interpretations of the experience, but rather of the universal and unanimous declaration on the part of *all* mystics, Western as well as non-Western, that the experience is of non-dual reality which is non-different from the mystic's true being and therefore ineffable. Let us now clarify — *not* describe — the mystical experience. When a mystic from a theistic tradition says he has experienced God, he is *not* saying that his experience is one in which he sees (perceives) God as an *object* (phenomenon). If one experiences God as an object, one should be able to *describe* God; such an experience is dualistic, since it is characterized by the subject-object (experiencer-experienced) distinction. But insofar as mystics themselves tell us that their experience, transcending the senses and the mind, is non-dualistic experience (devoid of any and all distinctions), it should be clear that when a mystic says he has experienced God he is not saying that he has experienced God as an object, as the other. In the mystical experience, then, the tripartite distinction, namely, the knower, the activity of knowing, and the known, characteristic of all dualistic experience (knowing through the senses and the mind), simply vanishes away; that is, in the mystical experience one's knowing and one's being are non-different, one and the same. This is the meaning of the mystical claim of the unity of non-dual ultimate reality and one's true being. In this mystical experience, there is neither the subject nor the object, there is just *ātman*, pure consciousness, consciousness *without* objects. This is the reason for the ineffability of the experience (pure consciousness defies any and all attempts to describe). Hence the Upaniṣadic teaching, "I am *Brahman*," "That thou art," and so on.

The ineffability of the non-dual experience is the reason mystics refuse to talk about their experience and prefer to remain silent: those who know It do not speak of It and those who speak of It do not know It; the Tao that can be named is not the real Tao, and so on.

It is precisely in the light of these considerations that Meister Eckhart, among the greatest of mystics, Western or non-Western, distinguished God from Godhead, and went on to exhort people seeking liberating knowledge to pray to God to rid them of Him, so that they can transcend all concepts, images, and projections of the non-dual reality (*Brahman, ātman*). God is a concept, an image, and a projection which holds one a captive, thereby preventing one from realizing the formless, nameless non-dual ultimate reality: man's last and highest parting is, when for God's sake, he takes leave of God (Eckhart), As the soul becomes more pure and bare and poor, and possesses less of created things, and is emptied of all things that are not God, it receives God more purely, and is more completely in him. It truly becomes one with God, and it looks into God and God into it, face to face as it were; two images transformed into one. Some simple folk think that they will see God as if he were standing there and they here. It is not so, *God* and I, we *are one* (Eckhart). Only to whom God is *present in everything* and who employs his reason in the highest degree and has enjoyment in it knows anything of true peace and has a real kingdom of heaven; the eye with which I see is the *same* eye with which God sees (Eckhart). Godhead is the ultimate non-dual reality (*Brahman*), non-different from one's true being (*ātman*, pure, objectless consciousness); and the great Islamic mystic (sūfī), Al Halaj, resoundingly proclaimed, "I am Allah and Allah is wherever I am." (It is appropriate to note here that Al Halaj was demanded by the Caliphate to recant and retract his allegedly blasphemous claim, "I am Allah"; and when he refused to do so, he was promptly burnt at the stake. Similarly, Eckhart was asked by the Vatican to appear and explain his seemingly blasphemous claim, "the eye with which I see is the same eye with which God sees." Eckhart prepared an answer and an explanation; however, to the good of the Church and the good of Eckhart he died a week or so before he was to appear before the Vatican). What all this goes to show is that most human beings, including leaders of religious organizations, are stuck at the dualistic level of understanding, and anyone who transcends all dualisms, through the mystical experience of the non-dual ultimate reality — Godhead — is regarded as a heretic and a purveyor of untruth and blasphemy. The examples of Al Halaj and Eckhart clearly show that mystical experience, as experience of the non-dual ultimate reality, is a common fund of human wisdom and hence found in all traditions, theistic, non-theistic, Western and non-Western alike. The desire for such an experience cannot be suppressed by any authorities. There have always been men and women, even from the dualistic-theistic traditions, who have had the mystical experience of the non-dual ultimate reality. The Upaniṣadic tradition is distinguished for its emphasis on the mystical experience; accordingly, it is the tradition which preserves, fosters, and promotes mysticism and mystical experience. It is also the tradition which encourages total freedom of inquiry, without any interference from any authorities. For, as has already been clarified several times, the Upaniṣadic teaching exhorts people never to settle for second-hand truth but discover the first-hand truth through their own direct and authentic mystical experience of the non-difference of the ultimate non-dual reality (*Brahman*) and one's true being (*ātman*), by earnestly and diligently pursuing the path(s) most suited to them. Thus, the Upaniṣadic teaching, by virtue of its emphasis on non-duality and its discovery through the non-dual mystical experience, is truly and triumphantly the longest surviving and the most eloquent and dedicated guardian, protector, preserver, and promoter of the purest, highest, and most sublime mysticism — in short, mysticism, *par excellence,* unsurpassed and unsurpassable. Being the crowning glory of mysticism, the Upaniṣadic teaching is in full accord with *all* mystical teachings, whether Western or non-Western. In the next and final chapter, I shall sum up the work and conclude it with some relevant and salient observations and remarks.

6

Concluding Remarks and Reflections

I AM sure the reader has discerned that the Upaniṣads are at once philosophical and religious works. They are philosophical works in that they raise the most profound questions concerning the whither and whence of the world, its nature and status, one's true being, and ultimate reality, and offer their answers founded in intellect illumined by intuition and intuition informed by intellect. They are religious works, not in the ordinary sense of the term "religious," but in the most profoundly mystical sense; whereas Western religious discourse revolves around God, that of the Upaniṣads revolves around ultimate reality. Yes, there is in the Upaniṣads discussion of God, as understood in all theistic traditions, Western or non-Western; but "God" here is to be understood in the sense of *Saguṇa Brahman* (ultimate formless and nameless non-dual reality *Brahman, ātman,* conceived of by frail and feeble human beings as having a form and a name, whom they worship, pray to, and ask for mercy, forgiveness, and grace). Ultimate reality is formless and nameless; and different peoples give different forms and names to this reality, each form and name being the products of a variety of factors, such as geographic, linguistic, economic, socio-political, and so on. Each group of people thinks that the form and name — the conception — given by its own tradition are the *true and correct* ones and it is its religious obligation to convert other peoples, with different forms and names for the *same* formless and nameless non-dual reality; if they resist conversion by persuasion, they should be converted by force and violence — the sword and the gunpoint. In this manner arise religious intolerance, dogmatism, fanaticism, and *exclusivism*, leading to religious wars and acts of unspeakable horror and cruelty, all committed in the name of their God(s). The Upaniṣadic tradition is unequivocally opposed to converting any people. The reason for this stance should be clear by now: the Upaniṣadic tradition, unlike almost all other traditions, clearly recognizes that different people give different forms and names to one and the same imperceivable and inconceivable non-dual reality; and it is therefore the height of ignorance and unwisdom to claim that one's own conception of the inconceivable is the true and correct one. If the ultimate non-dual reality is formless and nameless, how can anyone claim that the form and name given to it by one's own tradition are the correct form and name?

It is worthy of note that the answers given by the Upaniṣads to the different philosophical questions alluded to above are answers not grounded in any appeals to a God; rather, they are answers entirely grounded in the insights and experiences of the sages. Each person is exhorted by the sages to subject the answers to systematic examination and analysis, and not accept them on the basis of any authority. Each person should accept or reject the Upaniṣadic teaching in the light of his or her own inquiry and experience; for to accept any claim on the basis of authority, whether a book, a person, or an organization, no matter how lofty, exalted, and venerable, is to settle for second-hand truth, which is always open to the assault of doubt and consequently rejection. Only first-hand truth, truth certified by one's own authentic and direct experience, is worthy of the appellation "truth." For this reason, mysticism and mystical experience are at the very heart of the Upaniṣadic teaching.

The Upaniṣadic teaching is the earliest to distinguish between lower truths and the higher truth (*Muṇḍaka Upaniṣad*). The Upaniṣads (integral parts of the Vedas) are also unique in the whole world for their declaration that even the Vedas (sacred writings) are lower truth, since they are couched in language — percepts and concepts — which is through and through dualistic and hence incapable of capturing the non-dual reality, *Brahman* (*ātman*). In sharp contrast, other traditions, particularly the theistic Western traditions, claim their scriptures to be the word of God. The reason for this is that in these traditions the distinction between lower truths and the higher truth is conspicuous by its absence. Accordingly, these traditions put between the two covers of the same book (scripture) instructions as to how one should go about dealing with matters of the world — time-bound existence — and how to attain salvation. Matters pertaining to time-bound existence are necessarily governed by the fact of change, and as circumstances change, how one should go about time-bound existence also changes; in short, these traditions failed to distinguish philosophies of time and philosophies of eternity. In keen contrast, the Upaniṣadic tradition clearly distinguishes philosophies of time and philosophies of eternity; accordingly, in this tradition, there is the distinction between Dharmaśāstras (philosophies of time, which deal with matters pertaining to time-bound existence) and the Upaniṣads, philosophies of eternity, which deal with the timeless non-dual ultimate reality. The failure to draw the distinction between philosophies of time and philosophies of eternity — confounding lower truths and the higher truth — has had tragic consequences in the Western tradition, such as persecution, excommunication, Papal indulgences, exile, burning people at the stake, torture of the so-called heretics, and so on. Such things were never even heard of in the Upaniṣadic tradition; in this tradition, every person is free to interpret the sacred writings in his or her own way, there being no centrally constituted authority to tell anyone as to how he or she should interpret and understand the sacred writings. One can listen to others and learn from them, but no one can tell one, "If you do not accept and follow what I told you, you will go to hell." Freedom of thought and inquiry is taken for granted in the Upaniṣadic tradition. This is the reason for Hinduism's being an unorganized religion and tradition. This means that there has never been in the entire history of the tradition a central authority to dictate and control as to how one is to interpret and understand the sacred writings. Ultimate questions are too important and significant to be left for others to determine the answers. Each has do it on her or his own. Hence the centrality of mysticism in the Upaniṣadic tradition. Otherwise, one has only second-hand truth, which is no good, no matter how lofty and venerable a source it comes from.

The remarks made above concerning Western religious traditions — Judaism, Christianity, and Islam — are not to be construed as disrespecting and belittling these traditions; rather, they are to be understood as simply indicative of the fact that mysticism and mystical experience never occupied the central place in these traditions, unlike in the Upaniṣadic tradition. Western religious traditions are first and foremost devotional and hence dualistic traditions. Moreover, the Western religions have always been, for a number of historical circumstances, *organized* religions — religions with central authorities to tell people what they should believe and how they should conduct themselves. It is in the very nature of organized religions to have a uniform system of belief and conduct, zealously guarded, protected, propagated, and implemented by the central authorities; and, naturally enough, anyone whose belief and conduct are at variance with the official (orthodox) doctrines and codes only deserves to be declared a heretic and denounced and punished by the authorities. Strangely enough, when the authorities burn an alleged heretic at the stake, they tell you they have to do this — burning alive the heretic at the stake — in order to save his or her soul from eternal damnation. Murdering a person, in order to save him? (!) What went wrong? What went wrong is that people, under the control of authorities, are required to believe in the truth of certain concepts, images, and projections of the ultimate non-dual reality, imperceivable and inconceivable by the senses and the mind, and therewith certain doctrines — imaginative constructions of Reality, *vaikalpa;* and when someone wants to inquire and question, and thereby challenge the authorities, one will be seen as a heretic, one who deviates from the true and correct *conception* of the inconceivable non-dual, ultimate, reality, thereby direly in need of correction. If the alleged heretic resists correction and restitution, then he surely deserves to be punished, even by being burnt at the stake, in order for his soul to be saved.

Different religious traditions arose in different times and climes, each with its own *conception* of the inconceivable, ultimate, non-dual reality. But each tradition, by failing to distinguish between lower truths and the higher truth, thought and continues to think that the conceptions and doctrines of its own are the true and correct conceptions and doctrines. This is *avidyā* (ignorance), and its tragic consequences are dogmatism, intolerance, fanaticism, exclusivism, and acts of unspeakable horror and cruelty. The point of all these observations is that confounding the lower truths and the higher truth has grave consequences. In sharp contrast, one who truly comprehends the distinction between lower truths and the higher truth — and therewith between the imperceivable and inconceivable, non-dual, ultimate reality, on the one hand, and *conceptions* of the non-dual reality on the other, is a true mystic; for he has transcended all images, concepts, projections, and all doctrines — in a word, all dualities — and attained the highest realization: the non-difference of one's true being (*ātman*) and ultimate reality (*Brahman*).

What is remarkable, however, is that even in the theistic-dualistic organized traditions of the West, there always arose men and women who, through their mystical experience, transcending all conceptions and doctrines, acknowledged the non-difference of the ultimate non-dual reality and one's true being.

Some scholars distinguish two kinds of mysticism: extrovertive mysticism and introvertive mysticism. "Both are apprehensions of the One, but they reach it in different ways. The extrovertive way looks outward and through the physical senses into the external world and finds the One there. The introvertive way turns inward introspectively and finds the One at the bottom of the self, at the bottom of the human personality.

The latter far outweighs the former in importance both in the history of mysticism and in the history of human thought generally" (W.T. Stace, *The Teachings of the Mystics*, New York: Mentor, 1960, p. 15). Such a distinction, however, breaks down in regard to the Upaniṣadic teaching; for, as has been clarified several times now, the Upaniṣads resoundingly declare that the non-dual reality (*Brahman*) underlying the ever-changing external world is non-different from the non-dual reality (*ātman*) underlying the constantly changing internal world: "What is within us is also without. What is without is also within. He who sees difference between what is within and what is without goes evermore from death to death" (*Aitareya Upaniṣad*, III.i.3); "That which is the subtle essence — in that have all beings their existence. That is the truth. That is the Self. And that, O Svetaketu, That Thou art" (*Chāndogya Upaniṣad*, VI.x.3); and "The self who understands all, who knows all, and whose glory is manifested in the universe, lives within the shrine of the heart, the city of *Brahman*" (*Kaṭha Upaniṣad*, II.4.10). The central teaching of the Upaniṣads, *Brahman* and *ātman* are non-different, is none other than the proclamation of non-difference of extrovertive and introvertive mysticism. The Upaniṣadic teaching clearly shows that extrovertive mysticism and introvertive mysticism are not mutually exclusive; for it emphasizes that a true mystic is at once an extrovertive and introvertive mystic. Such a mystic, whether she looks outward or inward, finds the ultimate non-dual reality (*Brahman, ātman*).

In the light of the teaching of two kinds of knowledge and truth, let us now clearly list the following pairs, the first element of which belongs in the higher truth and the second in lower truths: Reality and appearance, *Brahman* and the world, *ātman* and *jīva* (empirical ego), *Nirguṇa Brahman* and *Saguṇa Brahman* (God, *Īśvara*), and *guru* and *puṇḍit* (scholar). There is the non-dual reality *Brahman* and its variety of manifestations — the world. There is the non-dual *ātman* and many *jīva*s (living beings, appearances of *ātman*). There is the non-dual reality and many conceptions of It — gods of different theistic traditions. There is the higher truth (*pāramārthika satya*) which transcends the senses and intellect and many lower truths (*vyāvahārika satya*), the product of the operation of the senses and mind. Before proceeding to clarify the terms *guru* and *puṇḍit,* a few observations on language are in order. Broadly speaking, we distinguish two kinds of use of language: the conceptual use and the non-conceptual use. In all rational-scientific inquiries, language is used conceptually; that is, here each concept has a clear meaning and referent. Thus, for example, "electron" has the same meaning and referent to all physicists; otherwise, physics as a body of objective knowledge becomes impossible. Non-conceptual use of language is dominant in poetry, scriptures, sacred writings, and religious works in general. When someone goes to study with a scholar (*puṇḍit*), the scholar teaches him the language, gets him to read the texts and commentaries, gives him examinations, and when the student's performance is satisfactory, the scholar lets him go. That is, the scholar's main aim is to enable the student to become a scholar in his own right; accordingly, the scholar's use of language is predominantly conceptual and informative. In keen contrast, when someone goes to study with a *guru,* an enlightened being, the *guru* employs language with great skill and dexterity in any manner he deems fit; sometimes he uses language conceptually and other times non-conceptually. The *guru*'s use of language is predominantly non-conceptual; his main purpose is not to provide the student some more information and another long list of facts, textual or otherwise, but rather to inspire the student and awaken and orient his mind to the quest for ultimate reality. In a word, his use of language is primarily evocative and only secondarily informative; accordingly the *guru* freely resorts to analogies, metaphors, figures of speech, mythic discourse, parables, and so on, and makes sure that the student does not take any of these things literally (conceptually). It is clear that, unlike the scholar (*puṇḍit*), the *guru* is primarily concerned with inspiring the student and awakening him to the quest for the non-dual ultimate reality, thereby radically transforming the student. We are all aware that Zen masters are adepts at non-conceptual use of language, as witness the *koan*s. The Zen master gives the student a *koan* and asks him to solve it; a *koan* is a riddle that cannot be resolved through any rational procedure. Every time the student comes up with an answer, the Zen master simply rejects the answer and asks him to go back and work on the *koan*. Examples of *koan*s are: What was your face like before you were conceived? What is the sound of one hand clapping? The point here is that, as the student tries harder and harder to solve the *koan*, his intellect becomes progressively exhausted and finally collapses, thereby making it possible for the student to experience in a flash of intuition the non-dual ultimate reality. Contrary to the widespread but uncritical belief that *guru*s, including Zen masters, reject language altogether, *guru*s use language to point to that which cannot be captured and expressed in language; that is, language is like a finger pointing at the moon, and the *guru*s exhort the student not to mistake the finger for the moon. And once one has been enabled to see the moon by pointing at it with a finger, neither the finger nor the pointing is necessary. The Upaniṣadic sages are among the most distinguished *guru*s. It would be a serious mistake to think that one and the same person cannot be both a scholar (*puṇḍit*) and a *guru*. The Upaniṣadic sages are not only great *guru*s but also great thinkers; and Śaṅkara, the founder of Advaita Vedānta, is a shining example of a *puṇḍit* and a *guru*.

Unlike in the Western traditions, in the Upaniṣadic tradition there has never been hostility, rivalry, and warfare among science, philosophy, and religion. The reason for this is twofold: first, there is in this tradition a clear understanding of the teaching of two kinds of knowledge and truth, the lower and the higher; and second, this tradition is not an organized tradition, with central authorities to exercise thought-control on the masses. Hence the insistence and emphasis in this tradition that each person discover the truth through his or her own direct experience. For this reason, mysticism occupies the central place in this tradition. In sharp contrast, in organized traditions mystics are always perceived as threats by the authorities and consequently mysticism is discouraged and one's giving one's assent to the proclaimed doctrines is central.

In the Upaniṣadic tradition, unlike in the Western traditions, science, philosophy, and religion form a continuum. When one pursues science far enough, one encounters philosophical questions, and when one pursues philosophy far enough, one encounters religious questions. We have shown in an earlier chapter that science itself points to a transcendent reality; how so? Science cannot, in principle, explain how and why there is a world at all. But there is indeed a world. Therefore the question as to how and why there is a world at all transcends not only science but all rational inquiries. In the Upaniṣadic tradition, science, philosophy, and religion, like art, are understood as manifestations of the creativity of the human spirit.

Conflicts among science, philosophy, and religion in the Western tradition are direct consequences of organized religions and therewith central religious authorities. (This is not to suggest that there never were religious conflicts in the history of India; there certainly were conflicts and animosities between militant Vaiṣṇavaites and Śaivaites, and Hindus and Muslims, but these were very infrequent and uncharacteristic of the Hindu tradition). Religious authorities interfered with the pursuit of rational-scientific inquiries. People had to fight battles against religious authorities in order to free themselves from the grips of these authorities. It is in this manner that free thinking and pursuit of science came about in the West about three centuries ago. And once thinkers freed themselves from the control of religious authorities, they naturally wanted to remain dissociated from religious authorities. In course of time, with the steady rise of rational-scientific pursuits, religion and scriptures themselves came under unrelenting scrutiny and criticism, eventually leading to heightened scepticism and the undermining of faith; and since the devotional path is the only path in Western religious traditions, it is only natural that once faith was undermined there was no other path to follow. When rational-scientific people rejected the answers given by their tradition to certain fundamental existential questions, they mistakenly thought that the questions themselves will thereby disappear. But the questions did not disappear and are staring into their faces for answers. These questions do not disappear and they have to be dealt with one way or another. Since the tradition did not provide any other path than the devotional, the sceptics did not have any other path; in this manner came about nihilism, meaninglessness, and philosophies of angst (anxiety) and the absurd. But why, in the first place, one might ask, religious authorities interfered with rational-scientific pursuits? The answer should by now be clear and straightforward: failure to distinguish between the higher truth and lower truths and therewith pitting the scriptures against scientific findings and treatises. Scientific treatises are always open to revision, modification, and sometimes outright rejection and replacement because they deal with time-bound existence; consequently, there is no room for finality in science. Scriptures are concerned with salvatory knowledge and it is a grave error to confound the higher and lower truths.

There is in the Upaniṣadic tradition absolutely no room for confounding lower and higher truths. However, many Westerners, particularly self-proclaimed rational-scientific thinkers, in the light of the history of their own tradition, fraught with hostility, animosity, and warfare between science and religion, uncritically think that such is the case in *all* civilizations and traditions and look upon religion everywhere with suspicion, contempt, and hostility. It is my earnest belief that I have shown in this work that such a view is wholly mistaken. Thus it is not at all uncommon for an Upaniṣadic Hindu to be at once a distinguished rational-scientific thinker and a practitioner of some form or other of *yoga* as a spiritual discipline. Rational-scientific inquiries have their proper place in enabling us to efficaciously deal with time-bound existence; but rational-scientific knowledge, belonging to the domain of lower truths and knowledge, lacks soteriological power. That is, it lacks the power to radically transform the human being into one of wisdom, freedom, peace, joy, and harmony, which can only come through mystical experience and therewith the realization of the non-difference of the ultimate non-dual reality and one's true being (*Brahman* and *ātman* are non-different, *Aham Brahmāsmi,* I am *Brahman, tat tvam asi,* That thou art). Let us again emphasize that the mystical experience can only come when one transcends *all* images, concepts, projections, and doctrines. This injunction to transcend all images, concepts, projections, and doctrines is the crowning glory of the Upaniṣadic teaching.

The methodology of the Upaniṣadic teaching is in full conformity with the spirit of rational-scientific inquiry. How so? Someone wishes to be a great scientist, say a physicist; what should she do? She should go to a great physicist and study under his guidance — learn the language of physics, the methods and procedures of observation and theory-construction, and do the experiments in order to confirm or disconfirm any claim made by a physicist. Just so, if someone "wishes to confirm or disconfirm the teaching of the Upaniṣadic sages, that someone should go and study under the guidance of a realized being, a *guru,* who will disabuse him of his mistaken views and ideas, and give him a procedure by which to test and confirm or disconfirm the teaching. One will then undertake systematic theoretical and experimental investigation, as per the teaching and procedures given by the *guru,* and confirm or disconfirm the truth of the teaching of non-duality (Advaita). This is exactly how things are done in scientific inquiry and investigation. Remember the Upaniṣadic exhortation that no one should accept a claim unless certified by one's own authentic, direct, and immediate experience?

I beseech the reader, particularly the Western reader, not to construe any remarks and observations I have made about the Western religious traditions as disrespectful and discourteous, but only as remarks and observations on historical facts. The mystics of the Western tradition are indistinguishable from those of the non-Western ones, including the Upaniṣadic. The import of my remarks and observations is that mysticism never occupied the central place in the Western traditions, unlike in the Upaniṣadic tradition; and I offer this work to people of all traditions, Western and non-Western alike, in the earnest and fervent hope of inspiring them to commit themselves, through study and practice, to the supreme mystical quest, by remaining in the traditions they have inherited.

Nothing could be a more fitting conclusion to this work than the following observations on the Upaniṣads by Arthur Schopenhauer, the great German philosopher, and Erwin Schrodinger, the great Austrian physicist, one of the founders of Quantum theory, and a Nobel Laureate: "The Upaniṣads provide the most rewarding and the most elevating reading the world has to offer. It has been the consolation of my life and will be my consolation when I come to die" (Schopenhauer, *Parerga und Paralipomena,* II [1888], p. 427). "One thing can be claimed in favour of the mystical teaching of the "identity" of all minds with each other and with the supreme mind — as against the fearful monadology of Leibniz. The doctrine of identity can claim that it is clinched by the empirical fact that consciousness is never experienced in the plural, only in the singular. Not only none of us ever experienced more than one consciousness, but there is also no trace of circumstantial evidence of this ever happening anywhere in the world" (Schrodinger, *What is Life? Mind and Matter,* New York: Cambridge University Press, p. 139). Further, "From the early great Upaniṣads the recognition *ātman=Brahman* (the personal self equals the omnipresent, all-encompassing, all comprehending eternal self) was in Indian thought considered, far from being blasphemous, to represent the quintessence of deepest insight into the happenings of the world. The striving of all the scholars of Vedānta was, after having learnt to pronounce with their lips, really to assimilate in their minds this grandest of all thoughts. . . . Consciousnesss is never experienced in the plural, only in the singular. . . . Consciousness is a singular of which the plural is unknown" (Schrodinger, *What is Life & Other Scientific Essays,* New York: Doubleday, pp. 86-87).

One last remark: The Upaniṣads teach that whosoever attains the knowledge of the ultimate non-dual reality *Brahman* (*ātman*) goes beyond good and evil. Many misunderstand this teaching as implying that one who realizes *Brahman* commits evil with impunity. Nothing could be farther from the truth. Good and evil, as we have seen, belong in the domain of duality, the world of the senses and intellect, time-bound existence. Good and evil are polar in the sense that there cannot be the one without the other, like mountains and valleys. How, then, is one to understand the Upaniṣadic proclamation that he who realizes *Brahman* goes beyond good and evil? Remember the exhortation of Christ that one should love one's neighbour as oneself? Christ did not give any reason for his exhortation; the Upaniṣads give the reason as to why one should treat one's neighbour as oneself: In one's true being as *ātman* (*Brahman*), one's neighbour is oneself; that is, one is non-different from one's neighbour. And since one always wants everything best for oneself, the realized being unfailingly wishes for everything best for his neighbour. That is, he will never do unto his neighbour what he does not want done unto himself. Thus the realized being experiences the joys and sorrows of his neighbour as his own. And since he who realizes *Brahman* also knows that time-bound existence — existence as *jīvas* — is governed by dualities, including that of good and evil, he always, unfailingly, does for his neighbour what in his best knowledge and belief is most conducive to the well-being of his neighbour. His actions are always actions with concern but absolutely no attachment. What governs his actions are purity of heart and motive, untainted by jealousy, greed, and selfishness — in short, all forms of egoism. Remember that there is no *other* for him who realizes the non-dual *Brahman* (*ātman*). This is the meaning of the Upaniṣadic declaration: He who realizes *Brahman* (*ātman*) has gone beyond good and evil.

Glossary of Sanskrit Terms

abhāva: non-existence, negation, absence

ācāra: conduct, discipline, observance

ācārya: great teacher, master

ādhāra: support

adharma: moral demerit

ādheya: the supported

adhyāsa: superimposition

adṛṣṭa: unseen power (*karma*)

adṛṣṭārtha: imperceivable objects

Advaita: non-dual(istic), a school of Vedānta

Agni: the Vedic god of fire

ahaṁkāra: egoism, ego-sense, sense of "I," "me," and "mine"

ajīva: non-soul, the inanimate

ākāśa: space, ether (substratum of sound in Nyāya-Vaiśeṣika metaphysics)

alaukika: extraordinary

āḻvār: one who through utter self-surrender and pure devotion has attained union with God; the term usually refers to the Vaiṣṇava poet-saints of south India

anādi: beginningless

ānanda: bliss

anantam: infinite

anavasthā: infinite regress

aṅga: organ, part

anitya: impermanent

antaḥkaraṇa: internal organ constituted of mind (*manas*), ego-sense (*ahaṁkāra*) and intellect (*buddhi, mahat*)

antarindriya: internal sense (mind)

aṇu: atom (the indivisible)

anumāna: inference

anupalabdhi: non-cognition (one of the six *pramāṇas* of Advaita Vedāntā)

aparā-vidyā: empirical, lower, mundane, relative knowledge (see *parā-vidyā*)

aparokṣa: immediate, direct, without the mediation of the senses

Āraṇyakas: Forest-treatises (that part of the Vedas primarily concerned with rites and ceremonies)

artha: means of life, wealth (one of the four *puruṣārtha*s), the non-perceptual, non-conceptual, intuitive knowledge of reality which the yogic aspirant seeks

arthāpatti: postulation (one of the six *pramāṇa*s of Advaita Vedānta)

āsana: discipline of the body consisting of steady and comfortable postures necessary for attaining one-pointedness and stillness of the mind (a limb of *aṣṭāṅga-yoga*)

asatkāryavāda: the theory that effect is not identical with (does not pre-exist in) cause (as opposed to *satkāryavāda*)

aṣṭāṅga-yoga: eight-limbed *yoga* (*yoga* as systematized by Patañjali in his *Yoga-Sūtras*)

asvatantra: the unfree

Atharva: one of the four Vedas

ātman: soul, the inmost Self which is eternal, nameless, and formless (not to be confused with the empirical ego)

avidyā: ignorance, nescience

aviveka: lack of discrimination (between the real and the unreal, and the true and the false)

baddha: the unfree, the bound

bāhya: external (as distinct from internal)

bhakti: devotion (to God)

bhakti-yoga: the *yoga* (path) of devotion

bhava: existence, becoming

bhāva: being, nature, reality, true condition

bhedābheda: identity-in-difference

bhoktṛ: enjoyer

Brahman: the eternal, nameless, formless ultimate reality of which the world of phenomena is manifestation

brāhmaṇa: (Brahmin; one of the four main caste divisions)

Brāhmaṇas: that part of the Vedas primarily concerned with rites, ceremonies, duties and conduct

buddhi: intellect (*mahat*)

citta: mind

darśana: vision (view) of truth and reality

dhāraṇā: concentration (a limb of *aṣṭāṅga-yoga*)

dharma: what holds together, the basis of all order, one of the four *puruṣārtha*s, law, moral merit

dhṛ: bearing, upholding, supporting, that which forms the foundation (root from which derives *dharma*)

dhyāna: meditation, contemplation (a limb of *aṣṭāṅga-yoga*)

dravya: substance

dravyatva: substantiality, state of being a substance

dṛṣṭānta: example, instance, an undisputed fact which illustrates a general rule, the third and last member of the Nyāya syllogism

dṛṣṭārtha: perceivable objects

duḥkha: suffering

Dvaita: dual(istic), a school of Vedānta

guṇa: constituent, quality, product, cosmic constituent (in Sāṁkhya metaphysics)

Indra: Vedic god of the heavens

Īśvara: God, creator, sustainer, and destroyer of the universe (see *Saguṇa-Brahman*)

Jaḍa: Prakṛti as unintelligent and unconscious

jāti: birth, class as determined by birth, universal (as distinct from particular), an unfair reply based on false analogy

jīva: animate substance, individual soul

jīvanmukta: he who is free while still alive

jñāna: knowledge, consciousness

jñāna-kāṇḍa: the part of the Vedas which deals with knowledge of ultimate reality (refers to the Upaniṣads)

***kaivalya*:** perfect independence, absolute freedom, *mokṣa*

***kāla*:** time

***kāma*:** desire, pleasure, passion (one of the four *puruṣārthas*)

***karma*:** action, effect of action

***karma-kāṇḍa*:** the part of the Vedas concerned with conduct, practice, and action — rituals and sacrifices (refers to the Saṁhitās, Brāhmaṇas, and Āraṇyakas)

***kartṛ*:** agent, doer

***kevala-jñāna*:** all-comprehensive (perfect) knowledge

***khaṇḍana*:** refutation

***laukika*:** ordinary, secular (as distinct from scriptural)

***līlā*:** sport, cosmic playfulness of *Brahman*

***mahat*:** intellect (*buddhi*, the first evolute of *prakṛti*)

***manana*:** reflection

***manas*:** mind

***mānasa*:** mental, internal

***māyā*:** cosmic illusion, cosmic ignorance, the power of *Brahman* by which *Brahman* manifests itself as the phenomenal world

***māyāvāda*:** Śaṅkara's doctrine of *māyā*, according to which the phenomenal world is neither real nor unreal but an appearance

Mīmāṁsā: revered thought, solution of problems by reflection and critical examination, a school of Vedānta

***mokṣa*:** absolute freedom (*kaivalya*) (one of the four *puruṣārthas*)

***muk*:** to release, to free (the root from which derives *mokṣa*)

***mukta*:** he who has attained *mokṣa*

***nāma*:** name

***nāma-rūpa*:** names and forms, concepts and percepts

Nāsadīya-Sūkta: the famous Ṛgvedic hymn of negation declaring that ultimate reality is indefinable, indescribable, imperceivable, etc.

***nididhyāsana*:** constant meditation which results in direct experience of truth and reality

***nirbījasamādhi*:** the state of *samādhi* which is free from all seeds of bondage, actual or potential

Nirguṇa Brahman: *Brahman* as ultimate reality transcending all perceptions and conceptions (names and forms)

nirṇaya: reliable and certain knowledge (about anything) obtained by any of the legitimate methods of knowledge (*pramāṇas*)

nirvikalpa: indeterminate

nirvitarka samādhi: that stage of yogic meditation in which the mind loses its essential subjectivity and consequently knows the object as it really is

nityamukta: one who is eternally free

niyama: self-culture which includes external and internal purifircation and moral virtues (a limb of *aṣṭāṅga-yoga*), the controlled

niyāmaka: controller

padārtha: category, object of experience, knowable

paramārtha-satya: higher, ultimate truth, absolute standpoint

parā-vidyā: higher knowledge (as distinct from lower knowledge), knowledge of *ātman*, of *Brahman*

pariṇāmavāda: the theory that when an effect is produced there is a real transformation of the cause into the effect (as distinct from *vivartavāda*)

Parjanya: Vedic god of the rain-cloud

prajñā: non-perceptual, non-conceptual, direct, intuitive insight into ultimate reality

Prakṛti: primal matter

pralaya: dissolution of the world into the primal, undifferentiated *Prakṛti*

pramā: valid presentative knowledge

pramāṇa: criterion (source, standard) of valid knowledge, way of knowing anything truly and objectively

prameya: knowable, object of true knowledge, reality

prāṇāyāma: control and regulation of breath (a limb of *aṣṭāṅga-yoga*)

prapatti: complete self-surrender to God

prātibhāsika: imaginary standpoint

pratyāhāra: the withdrawal of the senses from their objects (a limb of *aṣṭāṅga-yoga*)

pratyakṣa: direct, immediate (as distinct from *parokṣa*, mediate)

pratyaya: the totality of object(s) concentrated upon at any given time

Puruṣa: self (not to be confused with the empirical ego), spiritual substance

puruṣārthas: the goals (ends) of human life, four in number: *dharma, artha, kāma, mokṣa*

Puruṣa-Sūkta: the celebrated Ṛgvedic hymn declaring the organic unity of the universe (the oneness of all existence)

pūrva: prior, early

Pūrva-Mīmāṁsā: a school of Vedānta primarily concerned with providing philosophical justification for the Vedic ritualism

rajas: the active principle of existence, one of the three *guṇas* of *prakṛti*

ṛṣi: man of transcendent wisdom, sage

Ṛta: cosmic law (order), principle of righteousness, sacrificial correctness

rūpa: form

śabda: sound, testimony

saccidānanda: Pure Being, Pure Consciousness, Pure Bliss

ṣaḍāyatana: the six organs of knowledge

sādhana-catuṣṭaya: the fourfold discipline of Vedānta for the realization of ultimate reality

Saguṇa Brahman: Brahman conceived as having name and form *(Īśvara)* (as distinct from *Nirguṇa Brahman*)

sākṣin: *Ātman*, the witness self

Sāma: one of the four Vedas

samādhi: mind's absorption in the object of contemplation (the last and eighth limb of *aṣṭāṅga-yoga*)

sāmānya: generality, universal

samanyasa: cultivation of internal and external purity necessary for direct experience of ultimate reality (the first part of the *sādhana-catuṣṭaya*)

Saṁhitās: the parts of the Vedas dealing with *mantras* and hymns

Sāṁkhya (Sāṅkhya): an orthodox school of philosophy

saṁsāra: mundane existence, empirical reality, recurrent round of birth and death

saṁśaya: doubt, state of uncertainty

saṁskāra: kārmic impressions

saṁvṛtti: lower empirical standpoint

saṁvṛtti-satya: lower empirical truth

saṁyama: *dhāraṇā, dhyāna,* and *samādhi* taken together

sat: being (existence), good

satkāryavāda: the theory that effect is identical with (pre-exists in) cause (as opposed to *asatkāryavāda*)

sattva: one of the three *guṇas* of *prakṛti* (signifies everything pure, fine, and calm)

satya, satyam: reality, truth

savikalpa: determinate

savitarka-samādhi: the stage of yogic *samādhi* in which the three kinds of knowledge (*śabda, artha, jñāna*) exist in a mixed state

śeṣa: servant (devotee)

śeṣin: Lord (God)

siddha: one who has attained extraordinary powers as a result of yogic practice

siddhānta: theory, view, doctrine, conclusion

skandhas: components of human personality

sparśa: contact, touch

śravaṇa: attentive listening

sṛṣṭi: creation

sūkṣma: subtle, infinitesimal

svārtha: for oneself

svarūpa: essential form, internal form

svatantra: the free, the independent

tadvacana: his (their) word

tamas: one of the three *guṇas* of *prakṛti* (signifies stupor, laziness, stupidity, and inaction in general)

tanmātra: a simple or subtle element (as distinct from gross matter)

tarka: hypothetical argument by which one provides an indirect justification for a proposition by showing that its contradictory leads to absurdity (*reductio ad absurdum*)

tarkaśāstra: science of logic

tattva: truth, reality

tṛṣṇā: thirst, craving

upādāna: clinging

upādhi: limitation, limiting adjunct

upamāna: comparison (one of the six *pramāṇa*s of Advaita Vedānta)

Upaniṣad: secret teaching, sitting close to a teacher and receiving from him liberating knowledge, the concluding parts of the Vedas (concerned with knowledge of ultimate reality)

upāsanā: prayer, observance

uttara: posterior, later

Uttara-Mīmāṁsā: that branch of Vedānta whose chief concern is knowledge of ultimate reality (as distinct from Pūrva-Mīmāṁsā)

vāda: theory, doctrine, view, any discussion in which all arguments are explicitly and fully stated in the format of the Nyāya syllogism and every relevant *pramāṇa* and principle of logic cited

vaidika: pertaining to the Vedas, testimony of the Vedas

Vāyu: the Vedic god of air

vedanā: sense experience

Vedānta: concluding parts of the Vedas, the culmination of the Vedic wisdom, name of a group of philosophical schools with their foundations in the Vedas

Vedas: the most sacred scriptures of the Hindus

videhamukti: freedom from all bodies (gross as well as subtle), absolute freedom from all fetters of existence

vijñāna: consciousness

vikalpa: subjective forms (imaginative constructions) which have no empirical grounding and are therefore a priori

vinaya: discipline

Viśiṣṭādvaita: qualified non-dualism

vivartavāda: doctrine of apparent change — when an effect is produced, there is only apparent but no real transformation of the cause into the effect (as opposed to *pariṇāmavāda*)

vivekajñāna: discriminative knowledge

vyāvahārika: empirical (lower, mundane) standpoint

Yajur: one of the four Vedas

Yama (*yama*): Vedic god of death, and the first limb of *aṣṭāṅga-yoga,* consists of the cultivation of such qualities as non-violence, truthfulness, contentment

yoga: spiritual discipline and practice for self-realization and realization of ultimate reality

Bibliography

A. Vedic Hymns

Griffith, R.T.H., tr., *The Hymns of the Rigveda*, 2 vols., Banaras: E.J. Lazarus & Co., 1920-26.

Macdonell, A.A., tr., *Hymns from the Rigveda*, London: Oxford University Press, 1922.

Smith, H. Daniel, ed., *Selections from Vedic Hymns*, Berkeley: McCutchan Publishing Corporation, 1968.

Thomas, Edward J., tr., *Vedic Hymns*, London: John Murray, 1923.

B. The Upaniṣads

Deussen, Paul, *The Philosophy of the Upaniṣads*, tr. A.S. Geden, New York: Dover Publications, Inc., 1966.

Gambhirananda, Swami, tr., *Eight Upaniṣads, With the Commentary of Śaṅkarācārya*, vols. I & II, fourth impression, Calcutta: Advaita Ashrama, 1977.

Hume, R.E., tr., *The Thirteen Principal Upaniṣads*, New York: Oxford University Press, 1971.

Mahadevan, T.M.P., tr., *The Upaniṣads: Selections from the 108 Upaniṣads*, Madras: G.A. Natesan & Co., n.d.

Müller, F. Max, tr., *The Upaniṣads*, 2 vols., New York: Dover Publications, 1970.

Nikhilananda, Swami, tr., *The Upaniṣads*, 2 vols., New York: Harper & Brothers, 1951.

Prabhavananda, Swami, and Frederick Manchester, tr., *The Upaniṣads*, Hollywood: Vedānta Press, 1947.

Radhakrishnan, S., *The Philosophy of the Upaniṣads*, London: George Allen & Unwin, 1935.

———, tr., *The Principal Upaniṣads,* London: George Allen & Unwin, 1953.

C. Advaita

Alston, A. J., tr., *The Naiṣkarmyasiddhi of Śrī Sureśvara,* London: Shanti Sadan, 1959.

———, tr., *That Thou Art* (*From the Thousand Teachings of Śrī Śaṅkara*), London: Shanti Sadan, 1967.

Apte, V.M., tr., *Brahma-Sūtra-Śāṅkara-Bhāṣya,* Bombay: Popular Book Depot, I960.

Bhattacharyya, Kokileswar, *An Introduction to Advaita Philosophy,* Calcutta: University of Calcutta Press, 1924.

Bhattacharyya, Vidhushekhara, ed. and tr., *The Āgamaśāstra of Gauḍapāda,* Calcutta: University of Calcutta Press, 1943.

Date, Vinayak H., tr., *Vedānta Explained, Śaṅkara's Commentary on the Brahma-Sūtras,* 2 vols., Bombay: Bookseller's Publishing Co., 1954.

Datta, D.M., *The Six Ways of Knowing: A Critical Study of the Vedānta Theory of Knowledge,* Calcutta: University of Calcutta Press, 1960.

Deussen, Paul, *The System of the Vedānta, According to Bādarāyaṇa's Brahmāsūtras and Śaṅkara's Commentary,* tr., Charles Johnston., New York: Dover Publications, 1973.

Deutsch, Eliot, *Advaita Vedānta: A Philosophical Reconstruction,* Honolulu: East-West Center Press, 1969.

Deutsch, Eliot and J.A.B. van Buitenen, eds., *A Sourcebook of Advaita Vedānta.* Honolulu: University of Hawaii Press, 1972.

Devanji, Prahlad Chandrashekhas, tr., *Siddhāntabindu by Madhusūdanasarasvatī: A Commentary on the Daśaślokī of Śaṅkarācārya,* Gaekwad's Oriental Series, LXIV. Baroda: Oriental Institute, 1933.

Devaraja, N.K., *An Introduction to Śaṅkara's Theory of Knowledge,* Delhi: Motilal Banarsidass, 1961.

Gambhirananda, Swami, tr., *Brahma-Sūtra Bhāṣya of Śrī Śaṅkarācārya,* 3rd edn. Calcutta: Advaita Ashrama, 1977.

Gupta, Anima Sen, *Sāṁkhya and Advaita Vedānta: A Comparative Study,* Patna: Patna University Press, 1972.

Hasurkar, S.S., *Vācaspati Miśra on Advaita Vedānta,* Darbhanga: Mithila Institute, 1958.

Iyer, K.A. Krishnaswami, *Vedānta, or the Science of Reality,* Madras: Ganesh & Co., 1930.

Jagadānanda, Swāmi, tr., *Upadeśasāhasrī of Śrī Śaṅkarācārya* (*A Thousand Teachings*), Madras: Śrī Ramakrishna Math, 1961.

Johnston, Charles, tr., *The Great Jewel of Wisdom* (*Śaṅkara's Vivekachūdāmaṇi*), New York: Quarterly Book Department, 1925.

Joshi, Shanti, *The Message of Śaṅkara,* Ahmedabad: Lokbharati Publications, 1968.

Levy, John, *The Nature of Man According to Vedānta,* London: Routledge & Kegan Paul, 1956.

Mahadevan, T.M.P., *Gauḍapāda: A Study in Early Advaita,* Madras: University of Madras Press, 1954.

———, *The Philosophy of Advaita, with Special Reference to Bhāratītīrtha Vidyāraṇya,* London: Luzac & Co., 1938.

———, tr., *The Saṁhandha-Vārtika of Sureśvarācārya,* Madras: University of Madras Press, 1958.

Malkani, G.R., *Vedāntic Epistemology,* Amalner: The Indian Institute of Philosophy, 1953.

Mayeda, Sengaku, ed., *Śaṅkara's Upadeśasāhasrī,* Tokyo: The Hokuseido Press, 1973.

Mukharji, Nalini Mohan Sastri, *A Study of Śaṅkara,* Calcutta: University of Calcutta Press, 1942.

Murty, K. Satchidananda, *Revelation and Reason in Advaita,* New York: Columbia University Press, 1961.

Rao, K. Ramakrishna, *Advaita as Philosophy and Religion,* Mysore: University of Mysore Press, 1969.

Roy, S.S., *The Heritage of Śaṅkara,* Allahabad: Udayana Publications, 1965.

Sastri, Kokileswar, *An Introduction to Advaita Philosophy,* Calcutta: University of Calcutta Press, 1926.

———, *A Realistic Interpretation of Śaṅkara-Vedānta,* Calcutta: University of Calcutta Press, 1931.

Sastri, S.S., Suryanarayana, ed. and tr., *Vedāntaparibhāṣā by Dharmarāja Adhvarin*, Madras: The Adyar Library, 1942.

Sastry, A. Mahadeva, tr., *The Bhagavad-Gītā, with the Commentary of Śrī Śaṅkarācārya*, Madras: Ramaswamy Sastrulu & Sons, 1961.

Satprakāshānanda, Swami, *Methods of Knowedge (According to Advaita Vedānta)*, St. Louis: The Vedānta Society of St. Louis, 1972.

Sharma, B.N.K., *The Brahmāsūtras and Their Principal Commentaries: A Critical Exposition*, vol. 1, Bombay: Bharatiya Vidya Bhavan, 1971.

Shastri, Hari Prasad, tr., *Panchadashi: A Treatise on Advaita Metaphysics by Swami Vidyaranya*, London: Shanti Sadan, 1954.

Shastri, Prabhu Datt, *The Doctrine of Māyā in the Philosophy of the Vedānta*, London: Luzac & Co., 1911.

Shrivastava, S.N.L., *Śaṅkara and Bradley*, Delhi: Motilal Banarsidass, 1968.

Sircar, Mahendranath, *Comparative Studies in Vedāntism*, Bombay: Humphrey Milford, 1927.

Staal, J.F., *Advaita and Neo-Platonism: A Critical Study in Comparative Philosophy*, Madras: University of Madras Press, 1961.

Sundaram, P.K., *Advaita Epistemology with Special Reference to Iṣṭasiddhi.* Madras: University of Madras Press, 1968.

Thibaut, George, tr., *The Vedānta Sūtras of Bādarāyaṇa, with the Commentary by Śaṅkara*, 2 vols., New York: Dover Publications, 1970.

Urquhart, W.S., *The Vedānta and Modern Thought*, London: Oxford University Press, 1928.

Wood, Ernest, *The Pinnacle of Indian Thought: Verse-by-Verse Translation and Commentary in the Vivekachūdāmani of Śrī Śaṅkarācārya*, Wheaton, Ill.: The Theosophical Publishing House, 1971.

D. Viśiṣṭādvaita

Govindācārya, A., tr., *Śrī Bhagavad Gītā with Śrī Rāmānujācārya's Viśiṣṭādvaita Commentary*, Madras: Vaijayanti Press, 1898.

Gupta, Anima Sen, *A Critical Study of Rāmānuja.* Banaras: Chowkhamba, 1967.

Johnston, J., tr., *The Vedāntatattvasāra Ascribed to Rāmānujācārya*, Banaras: E.J. Lazarus & Co., 1898.

Krishnamachary, Pandit V., and M.B.A. Narasimha Iyengar, *Concise Viśiṣṭādvaita Commentary on the Brahma-Sūtras of Bādarāyaṇa*, Wheaton, Ill.: The Theosophical Publishing House, 1953.

Krishnamacharya, V., ed., *Vedāntasūtra of Rāmānuja*. Wheaton, Ill.: The Theosophical Publishing House, 1971.

Raghavachar, S.S., *Śrī Rāmānuja on the Gītā*, Mangalore: Śrī Ramakrishna Ashrama, 1969.

Rangacharya, Malur Rao, and Varadaraja Aiyangar, tr., *The Vedānta-Sūtras with the Śrī-Bhāṣya of Rāmānujācārya*, Madras: The Brahmavadin Press, 1919.

Sampatkumar, M.R., tr., *The Gītā Bhāṣya (of Rāmānuja)*, Madras: Rangacharya Memorial Trust, 1969.

Srinivasachari, P.N., *The Philosophy of Bhedābheda*, Madras: The Adyar Library, 1950.

———, *The Philosophy of Viśiṣṭādvaita*, Madras: The Adyar Library, 1943.

———, *Rāmānuja's Idea of the Finite Self*, Calcutta: Longmans, Green & Co., 1928.

Thibaut, George, tr., *The Vedānta Sūtras with the Commentary of Rāmānuja*, Oxford: Clarendon Press, 1904.

Van Buitenen, J.A.B., *Rāmānuja on the Bhagavadgītā*, Delhi: Motilal Banarsidass, 1968.

Varadachari, K.C., *Śrī Rāmānuja's Theory of Knowledge*, Tirupati: Tirumalai-Tirupati Devasthanams Press, 1943.

E. Dvaita

Krishnaswamy Rao, B.A., *Outlines of the Philosophy of Śrī Madhvācārya*, Tumkur, 1951.

Maitra, Sushil Kumar, *Madhva Logic*, Calcutta: University of Calcutta Press, 1936.

Nagaraja Rao, P., *Epistemology of Dvaita Vedānta*, Wheaton, Ill.: The Theosophical Publishing House, 1972.

Raghavendrachar, H.N., *Dvaita Philosophy and Its Place in the Vedānta*, Mysore: University of Mysore Press, 1941.

Sarma, Nagaraja, *The Rein of Realism in Indian Philosophy: Exposition of Ten Works by Madhva*, Madras: The National Press, 1937.

Subba Rao, S., *The Bhagavad-Gītā (Translation and Commentary in English According to Śrī Madhvācārya's Bhāṣya)*, Madras: The Minerva Press, 1906.

———, tr., *Vedānta-Sūtras with the Commentary of Śrī Madhvācārya*, Tirupati: Śrī Vyasa Press, 1936.

F. Related Works

Beardsley, Monroe C., ed., *The European Philosophers from Descartes to Nietzsche, with Introductions Commentaries, and Notes*, New York: The Modern Library, Random House Inc., 1960.

Blakney, Raymond B., tr., *Meister Eckhart: A Modern Translation*, New York: Harper & Row, 1941.

Forman, Robert K.C., ed., *The Problem of Pure Consciousness: Mysticism and Philosophy*, New York: Oxford University Press, 1990.

Hariharānanda Āraṇya, Swāmi, *Yoga Philosophy of Patañjali (Containing his Yoga aphorisms with Vyāsa's commentary)*, tr., P.N. Mukerji with a Foreword by Swami Gopalananda, Albany, N.Y.: State University of New York Press, 1983.

Koller, John M., *The Indian Way*, New York: Macmillan, 1982.

Miller, Barbara Stoller, tr., *The Bhagavad-Gītā: Kṛṣṇa's Counsel in Time of War*, New York: Bantam Books, 1986.

Puligandla, Ramakrishna, *Fundamentals of Indian Philosophy*, rev. edn., New Delhi: D.K. Printworld (P) Ltd., 1997.

———, *Jñāna-Yoga: The Way of Knowledge (An Analytical Inter pretation)*, rev. edn., New Delhi: D.K. Printworld (P) Ltd., 1997.

———, *Reality and Mysticism*, New Delhi: D.K. Printworld (P) Ltd., 1997.

Schopenhauer, Arthur, *Parerga und Paralipomena*, II, 1888.

Schrodinger, Erwin, *What is Life and Other Scientific Essays*, Garden City, N.Y.: Doubleday, 1956.

Srinivasa Rao, *Advaita: A Critical Investigation*, Bangalore: Indian Philosophy Foundation, 1985.

Stace, W.T., *The Teachings of the Mystics*, New York: Mentor, 1960.

Torwesten, Hans, *Vedānta: Heart of Hinduism,* Adapted by Loly Rosset from a translation from the German by John Phillips. New York: Grove Press Inc., 1991.

Venkatesananda, Swami, tr., *The Supreme Yoga: A New Translation of the Yoga Vāsiṣṭha,* vols. I & II, Elgin, South Africa: The Chiltern Yoga Trust, 1976.

"WHO," *Maha Yoga: The Upaniṣadic Lore in the light of the teachings of Bhagavan Śrī Ramana,* Tiruvannamalai: Śrī Ramanasramam, 1973.

Wilber, Ken, *The Spectrum of Consciousness,* Wheaton, Ill.: Quest Books, 1977.

Wolters, Clifton, tr., *The Cloud of Unknowing and Other Essays,* Translated into Modern English with an Introduction, New York: Penguin Books, 1985.

Zimmer, Heinrich, *Philosophies of India,* ed., Joseph Campbell, Bollingen Series, Princeton: Princeton University Press, 1969.

Index

absolute, 73, 75
adhyāsa, 63-64
Advaita Vedānta, 23
advitiyam, 27
Agni (fire), 2, 4
Aitareya, 9, 17, 116
Al Halaj, 109-10
ānanda, 93
anta, 9
aparā-vidyā, 17
apauriṣeya, 2
appearances, 53
Āraṇyakas, 1, 3-4
asat, 27-28
ātman, ix-x, 14-21, 24
avidyā, 61-62, 84, 87

Bādarāyaṇa, 24, 56
bhakti-yoga, 95
Bible, 85
Big-Bang, 83
bondage, 20
Bṛhadāraṇyaka, 9, 15, 17
Brahman, 11-21, 24
Brāhmaṇas, 2-4
Buddhism, xiii

categorial framework, 6, 9, 70-73, 75-76
Ch'an Buddhism, xiii
Chāndogya, 9, 12, 17, 116
chaos, 4
celā, ix, x
China, xiii, xvii
cit, 93
Christian, xiii, 1
consciousness, 19
  mystical, 7
  pure, 17
  religious, 3
cosmology, 84

Descartes, 47, 48
dharma, 86
Dharmaśāstras, 84-86
duḥkha, 78

Eckhart, Meister, 109-10
eternal truth, 9

Europe, xvii
evil, 123

forest treatises, 3
freedom, 17

God, 1, 28, 55, 89-91
good, 123
guru, 19, 117-18

henotheism, 4
here and now, 19
higher knowledge, 17-18
higher truth, 79

immortality, 19
India, xiii, 9
Indra (thunder), 2
infinite, 16
Īśa, 9, 11
Islamic, xiii, 1
Īśvara, 89-91

jaḍa, 16
Japan, xiii, xvii
Jewish, xiii, 1
jīva, 14, 38, 48, 49
jīvanmukta, 19, 92
jñāna-kāṇḍa, 2
jñāna-yoga, 102

kaivalya, 19
karma-kāṇḍa, 2
karma-yoga, 97
Kaṭha, vii-xi, 17-18, 20, 67, 116
Kena, 12-13, 17
knowledge, 17-18
  higher, 17-18
  lower, 17, 19
  sacred, 1

living-free, 19
lower knowledge, 17, 19
lower truth, 79

Madhva, 24
*mahāvākya*s, 17
Māṇḍūkya, 9, 41, 43, 48
*mantra*s, 18
māyā, 61-62
Mitra (Sun), 2
mokṣa, 17, 93-93
monotheism, 7
Müller, Max, 4
Muṇḍaka, 9, 12, 18-20, 69, 84, 112
mystic, 80
mysticism, xiii

Naciketās, vii-ix
nāma, 77
Nāsadīya-Sūkta, 6
Nirguṇa Brahman, 88-91, 116

Oṁ, ix, 20

panentheism, 6

pantheism, 6
paradigm, 73
pāramārthika-satya, 88, 106
parā-vidyā, 17
Parjanya (rain), 2
perceptual–conceptual framework, 71
phenomena, 53
polytheism, 4, 7
prāṇa, 13, 16, 92
prapatti, 96
puṇḍit, 117-118
puruṣa, 5-6
Puruṣa-Sūkta, 5

raja-yoga, 100
Rāmānuja, 24
Reality, 7, 53
  supreme, 5
  ultimate, 3, 7
ṛṣis, 16-18
rūpa, 77
ṛta, 4

Saccidānanda, 19, 67
Saguṇa Brahman, 88-91, 111, 116
Saṁhitās, 2
Śaṅkara, 23, 54, 56, 64, 73, 104, 118
sat, 27-28, 81, 93
Schopenhauer, Arthur, 122
Schrodinger, Erwin, 122
self, 17-18, 20
smṛti, 1
Sri Ramakrishna, 21
śruti, 1
sublation, 54
Svetāśvatara, 88

Taoism, xiii
Tat, 13
Tat tvam asi (That thou art), 17
Ten Commandments, 85
transcendental deduction, 70, 73-74
Transcendental Meditation, xiii
truth, xiv, 1, 17
eternal, 9
Turīya, 48-51

ultimate reality, 3-4, 6
union, 107
unity, 5-6, 107
U.S.A., xvii
unreality, 54
Upaniṣads, 2, 9
  Aitareya, 9, 17, 116
  Bṛhadāraṇyaka, xi, 9, 15, 17
  Chāndogya, 9, 12, 17, 116
  Īśa, 9, 11
  Kaṭha, vii-xi, 17-18, 20, 67, 116
  Kena, 9, 12-13, 17
  Māṇḍūkya, 9, 41, 43, 48
  Muṇḍaka, 9, 12, 18-20, 69, 84, 112
  Praśna, 9
  Śvetāśvatara, 88

Taittirīya, 9, 13

Vāyu (air), 2
Vedānta, xiii, 9
Vedas, 1, 2
Atharva, 2
Ṛg, 2, 4, 6
Sāma, 2
Yajur, 2
Parts of each Veda, 2
Āraṇyakas, 2
Brāhmaṇas, 2
Saṁhitās, 2
Upaniṣads, 2
Vedic Āryans, 9
vyāvahārika satya, 88

Yama, Lord, vii-x, 4
Yoga, xiii
Yoga-Sūtras, 101

Zen Buddhism, xiii, 118